Why?

Why?

Why Evil?
Why Suffering?
Why Death?

Russell Stannard

A LION BOOK

Published by
Lion Publishing plc
Mayfield House, 256 Banbury Road,
Oxford OX2 7DH, England
www.lion-publishing.co.uk
ISBN 0 7459 5122 8

First edition 2003
10 9 8 7 6 5 4 3 2 1 0

A catalogue record for this book is available
from the British Library

Typeset in 11/14 Baskerville

Printed and bound in Great Britain by
Cox and Wyman Limited, Reading

Contents

Introduction

Then the Lord answered Job out of the storm. He said: 'Who is this that darkens my counsel with words without knowledge?'
JOB 38:1–2

If the world was created by God, how come it is in such a mess? Had we been in charge, it is surely most unlikely we would have chosen a world like this one.

Take evil for a start: people cheating, lying, stealing, committing murder; children being sexually abused and bullied; innocent passers-by mugged in the streets or blown up by terrorist bombs; nations waging war on each other; and the ever-present threat of nuclear annihilation.

Then there is suffering that arises not from deliberate evil acts but from natural disasters: floods, earthquakes, volcanic eruptions, avalanches, droughts and disease – nature just doing its thing, following the normal course of events, no one's fault – suffering due to the way the world is.

Finally there is death. Doesn't the fact that one day we must die conclusively demonstrate that life is ultimately pointless; it has no lasting value?

Perhaps there is no God; the world somehow came into existence on its own. Humans are just an accident of nature. There is no purpose to life.

Things just happen to be the way they are, and we have to put up with it. Some people are resigned to that being the answer. To them it seems the only honest attitude to take.

But that is not how I and many others see it. We are convinced that there is a God – a God who created the universe and ourselves; he is the source of all existence. All-powerful and all-knowing, God is to be found everywhere in space and time, and also beyond the confines of the physical universe. God is good. He created us so that we might enter into a loving relationship with him. Those of us who are Christian believe further that he showed his own love for us in a very direct way by sending into the world his Son, Jesus, to share in our human life. Indeed, if we were allowed just one word to sum up the essence of God's character, that word has to be 'love'.

Which, of course, confronts us with the question we started with: if that is how we see God, why is the world the way it is? Why is there evil, suffering and death? How is it possible to square the harsh realities of life with a God of love?

It is an age-old problem, dating back to ancient Greek and Hebrew Old Testament times; many have wrestled with it. Do I have the answer? No, I do not – no clear-cut, pat answer. Nobody does. We are up against a mystery. By 'mystery', we do not mean a puzzle or a riddle with some neat solution, and all we have to do is be clever enough to find that solution. By 'mystery', we mean something that lies (and will always lie) beyond the complete grasp of the human mind.

That being so, what more is there to be said? Some hold there is nothing more to be said; we are called upon 'to have faith'. And to some extent they are right; we do have to have faith and trust that God knows best. But for myself and others, this in itself is not sufficient. To give up that easily is to invite the criticism that we are being intellectually dishonest – holding beliefs that plain common sense proves to be false.

While in no way denying the element of mystery, or the need for us ultimately to have faith, I do believe there are certain things that can be said about the problems of evil, suffering and death that might be helpful. At the very least, they demonstrate matters to be more subtle and complex than we might at first think.

Although the problem has been around for a long time, one thing has changed since the days it was first posed: science. Our scientific understanding of the world and of ourselves has been transformed. Without in any way claiming that science is likely to come up with the answer when all else has failed, I do think that scientific thinking can at certain points add depth to the discussion.

And that is what this book sets out to do. It attempts to provide an accessible introduction to the traditional arguments that have been formulated over the years, but at the same time, incorporates insights from a contemporary, scientific perspective.

I don't expect you to go along with everything

I shall be saying. Of course not. You have to decide for yourself what your own responses should be to the questions raised. But I would like to think that as we go along, you will come to recognize, if you do not already, that belief in a loving God does not have to be blind. Though we cannot grasp the whole picture – this side of the grave at any rate – we are able to glimpse enough of it to accept that *somehow* it could make sense.

In what follows, you will find I have split up the problem into three component questions: Why evil? Why suffering? and Why death? As will become evident, such a separation of the issues is somewhat artificial, the topics being so closely interlinked. Nevertheless, focusing on the three themes in this order does, I believe, make our task somewhat more manageable.

PART I

Why
Evil?

I said earlier that if we had been in charge of making the world, it is unlikely it would have turned out like this one. So what sort of world would we have chosen to create? What kind of thinking would we have built into its design?

The answer is pretty obvious. We would want any living things we created to be happy. That surely is the root of our quarrel with God: suffering, evil and the thought of impending death make us unhappy. Why would anyone want to produce creatures who had to live out sad and miserable lives? We would want our creatures to enjoy themselves – to live full and rewarding lives. Isn't the pursuit of happiness enshrined in the American Declaration of Independence as one of our rights? Happiness is surely a 'Good Thing'.

But how is that to be achieved? What makes for happiness?

Buying Happiness

To judge from the success of the lottery, and the popularity of TV shows such as *Who Wants to Be a Millionaire?*, one might think that happiness was primarily about gaining material possessions – having plenty of money. So why not a world where everyone has everything they could possibly want? Not only would that make people happy, it would have the added bonus of doing away with much of the evil we find in the world. If one already has everything one could possibly want, what would be the point of stealing from others, or mugging, killing or cheating them? At a stroke, we eliminate all jealousy and bitterness. With no motive for resorting to evil acts, everyone would be free to be kind and loving towards each other.

If God is all-powerful, presumably there was nothing to stop him making the world along those lines. So why didn't he?

By way of answer, let us consider those who come closest to that kind of ideal state: rich, well-off people. From what one reads about them in newspapers and magazines, they do not appear to be particularly happy. Though some are undoubtedly blessed with a generous spirit, too often the rich strike us as mean, spoilt and self-centred – slaves to their possessions. Not that one can altogether blame them. 'To suppose, as we all suppose, that we could be rich and not behave the way the rich behave, is supposing that we could drink all day and stay sober,' the American essayist Logan Pearsall Smith once warned.

Which is not to say that one has to go to the opposite extreme and claim that having possessions is a 'Bad Thing'. Much of the misery in the world is caused by people being hungry and having no proper home. We all need a certain minimum level of food, warmth and shelter. But we are not talking about that; we are talking of people having *everything* they want; we are going way, way beyond mere survival levels. If we really intend to make it pointless to steal, everyone has to already have everything they could possibly desire: the fastest sports car, the latest video games, the biggest TV screen, the most advanced hi-fi and so on.

It is here we come across something very strange. Survey after survey shows that above a certain minimum standard of living, extra wealth does *not* bring happiness. Young people, still looking forward to having all the goodies, find this hard to believe. But it is a fact of life that the progressive accumulation of material possessions and the attainment of an ever-increasing standard of living, leads to disappointment.

There is, of course, a certain buzz to buying something new and owning it for the first time. But the novelty quickly wears off. 'Possessions are generally diminished by possession,' said Nietzsche. We soon find ourselves taking whatever it is for granted; it becomes absorbed into the accepted baseline; our attention transfers to the next item on our list of wants.

There is a simple equation:

Happiness = achievement/expectation

The trouble is that as we achieve and amass more, so our ideas as to what we are entitled to also increase – in step – leaving the left hand side of the equation unchanged. No matter how high our standard of living, there is always someone who has even more than us. 'Much will have more,' as American philosopher–poet Ralph Waldo Emerson succinctly put it.

Let me give you an example. When I was

young, I used to play 'tuppenny ha'penny football'. The 'ball' was a small coin, the two 'footballers' were larger coins. I and my opponent took turns to flick our footballer-coin with our pocket combs so as to hit the ball-coin – aiming of course to score a goal. It was a game of real skill. Hours of fun, and once the matches were over, the coins and the combs went back into our pockets; it hadn't cost us a penny. These days it isn't like that. It is Playstation – or Playstation 2 – or is it 3 or 4 now? I am amazed as to how realistic today's video games have become (and horrified by their cost). And all for what? As far as I can see, these highly priced video games do not appear to give their players any more fun than I got from my tuppenny ha'penny version of the game.

If it is true that ever-increasing wealth does not buy happiness, why do we still strive to be better off? It seems the answer has something to do with competition. The attraction lies not so much in the goods themselves, as in having something other people do *not* have. One child has Playstation; but another has Playstation 2. One teenager wears a Gap T-shirt, another an Armani. It is a game that is continued into adult life – only with bigger and more expensive items: the size of one's house, the district where one lives, the make and age of the car, off-the-peg versus designer clothes, status at work and so on. Competition – keeping up with the Jones's. And the most effective way of proving your worth? To be paid lots of money and to buy expensive things.

The trouble is, where competition is concerned, someone has to lose – and be unhappy.

So what do we conclude? Is it really the case that one cannot buy happiness? Were the findings of those surveys to be trusted? If you still have doubts, take a look at suicide rates. Countries with the highest standards of living tend to be those that also have the highest suicide rates. For as long as one is in the position of reckoning that someday one will be a lot better off than now, it is easy to assume that once that happens one will be happier; it is something to look forward to. The trouble is, once people are better off, they discover this was an illusion; they are no happier; they feel let down. And all too often this loss of hope leads to suicide.

I detect something of the same kind of disappointment in people's attitude towards science these days. In the 1950s, when I was a university science student, scientists were highly respected and valued. The nation's economy had been torn apart by the Second World War, and scientists were looked up to as the ones who would restore and improve the standard of living – and make everyone a lot happier in the process. As a budding scientist I did not have to do the two years of military service that all other young men of my age had to do; scientists were too important for that! And sure enough, in due course, scientific advance delivered the goods: TVs, washing machines, tumble driers, CDs, mobile phones, microwave ovens, computers and so on. The standard of living today is unbelievably higher than it was when I was a young man. And yet, as some of us who have lived through the changes know to our cost, and those surveys confirm, people as a whole are no happier now than they were then. More comfortable, yes; we would not want to turn the clock back having experienced the conveniences of modern living. But as far as happiness is concerned, the deep-down, fulfilling type of happiness that promotes contentment and a sense of genuine achievement, no; that has eluded us. Perhaps this is why scientists seem no longer to be so highly regarded as once they were; we produced the goods, but the goods failed to deliver the happiness promised.

So what am I saying? The pursuit of happiness is doomed? Not necessarily, as long as we accept, along with Rabbi Hyman Schachtel, that 'happiness is not having what you want, but wanting what you have'. Moreover, we need to draw a distinction between superficial happiness, or pleasure, on the one hand, and deep contentment and fulfilment on the other. True happiness has to be sought in the satisfaction of our deepest desires. These seem more to be bound up with the meaning and purpose of life and the forming of loving relationships – of feeling valued for one's own sake, rather than for what one possesses, and in turn valuing others. 'Men can only be happy when they do not assume that the object of life is happiness,' observed George Orwell.

So we seem to have got off on the wrong foot by assuming that happiness (happiness supposedly rooted in material possessions) ought to have been made God's number-one priority in designing the world. Perhaps his choice of love rather than happiness as the all-important, overriding design principle was not such a bad one.

Being in Love

But first, we need to be clear what we mean by 'love'. For many, the word conjures up the idea of 'being in love'. Boy tells girl he is in love with her. She is thrilled; it's a wonderful feeling; she is happy. That being so, ought he not to make other girls happy too? Perhaps he should tell all the girls he meets, one by one, that he is in love with them as well. They too would be delighted (assuming he is a desirable young man). That way, everyone is happy. Until, of course, the girls compare notes and find out what he has been up to. Then they all feel let down. Why?

To quote George Orwell once more: 'To an ordinary human being love means nothing if it does not mean loving some people more than others.' Being in love is a kind of love that has to be exclusive. It can lead to two people wanting to spend the rest of their lives together in a way that they would not want to be spending it with anyone else. So an important feature of this kind of love is that one is picked out as being special – in that person's eyes at any rate. In other words, an element of competition has crept in again. The fact that you have been picked and others haven't can lead to others being disappointed. Or perhaps you are the one in the position of having been rejected by someone who has shown a preference for someone else. It can be a painful, unhappy experience. No, you can't experience the joy of being in love without also running the risk of experiencing the pain of rejection.

So if we are to seek happiness through love, rather than through the accumulation of material possessions, that being-in-love type of love cannot be the one we have in mind.

Universal Love

'In real love, you want the other person's good. In romantic love, you want the other person.' That is how the American writer Margaret Anderson draws the distinction between the type of love we have been talking about and another kind – the kind referred to in the Bible when it speaks of 'love your neighbour as yourself'. It is a love that has more to do with friendship, being good to others, respecting them, helping them out, always being kind and considerate. How about a world in which everyone loves everyone else in that sense – a world in which everyone also loves their Creator God?

A world of universal love and fellowship would be a world without evil. Could such a thing be possible? I don't see why not. If God had been so minded, he could have produced creatures who only ever behaved well and considerately – creatures who lived in perfect harmony. It was a possibility. But of course, such perfect creatures would not be people like you and me. People like you and me cannot be trusted always to choose to do the right thing. No, if these imaginary creatures were never to do evil acts, that could only be because they were incapable of doing evil acts. They would have to be pre-programmed in some way to do the right things – just like computers. If they were always to choose the right thing, without exception, then they would have no choice. And if they had no choice, they would have no free will; they would be no different from robots.

Free Will

That is not how it is with us. We value our freedom, our ability to decide for ourselves what we shall do with our lives, what we stand for. We are responsible for ourselves and our actions, and that's the way we want it to be. And that is also integral to God's plan for us. God has given us free will. Why? In order for love to be real, it cannot be pre-programmed or forced into us; it has to be freely offered. For God to give us the opportunity of freely offering him our love and devotion, he had to be prepared to live with the possibility that some of his creatures would exercise that freedom in other ways. God, of course, wants us to choose wisely and be good like he is. He wants all of us to behave so. But in giving us a choice, he opens up the possibility that we might not do as he wishes; we might turn our backs on him, the source of all goodness. And in turning our backs on him, we become more inclined to embrace the opposite, which is evil. Turning away from God, denying that he even exists, we fail to recognize that we are all children of a common father – a heavenly Father. We might still respect and love others as sharing a common humanity with us, but we fail to recognize each other as the brothers and sisters for whom we should be caring in the same special way as we would care for blood relatives.

In choosing love to be the guiding principle governing the nature of the created world, God had to bow to the inevitable and give us free will. That was something he had to do, knowing that the giving of such freedom would permit evil to enter into his creation. It was a terrible price to pay.

So am I saying God created evil at the same time as he created love? No. He created love – and love alone. But in doing so, he created the possibility of evil. It is we who are to blame for making evil a reality. This we do through the misuse of that God-given freedom.

And I really do mean 'we'. I am not talking about some evil people 'out there' different from you and me. Where evil is concerned it is at most only a matter of degree.

The fact that one must not try to draw clear-cut distinctions between people was brought home forcefully to me in prison. I had been asked to deliver a talk. The audience, I had been told, would consist of thirty-five murderers. I don't recall exactly what I had expected them to be like, but I certainly did not anticipate that they would appear so normal and ordinary. They had even helped bake the cakes we had at teatime. I needed reminding of William Hazlitt's remark, 'A wonder is often expressed that the greatest criminals look like other men. The reason is that they are like other men in many respects.' And according to Gavin Ewart, 'Bad men do what good men only dream.'

No, we are all evil in so far as there are times when each one of us, without exception, fails to live up to the true nature God intended for us. Jesus set the standard: 'Be perfect even as your heavenly Father is perfect.' This meant going further than the basic ten commandments. It was not sufficient merely to refrain from committing adultery; entertaining lustful thoughts was just as bad; not only should one not kill, one should not even be angry with another. Against such criteria we are all surely guilty.

Evil as an Illusion?

In saying that the responsibility for creating evil lies with us rather than with God, I am of course assuming that there is such a thing as evil. I should perhaps point out that there are those who hold that evil is nothing but an illusion; it has no reality. They deny that two opposites exist: goodness and evil. According to this view, only goodness exists; evil is merely the absence of goodness.

This is to regard evil in much the same way as we understand 'darkness'. Darkness is an absence of light. What is real is light, not darkness. 'Cold' is another of these negative qualities. In a sense, there is no such thing as coldness. Heat? Yes. Heat is the energy of molecules jiggling about, or the energy of heat rays coming from the sun or a fire. Coldness is merely the absence of heat.

If evil can be thought of in this way, as just another of these negative quantities, then we can stop worrying about who created it. No one did. What is created is goodness – and only goodness.

A pretty neat way of getting out of the problem, I think you'll agree. Neat, yes, but hardly satisfying. To speak of evil as simply an absence of goodness makes me uneasy. Such talk strikes me as not doing justice to the sheer force of evil. To regard something like evil as simply the absence of its opposite, underestimates its strength.

This is true even of 'cold'. Though intellectually we might argue that cold is nothing but the absence of heat, that is not how we subjectively experience it. We experience it as though it were something positive in its own right. We talk of a 'biting wind'; we talk of putting on clothes in order to 'keep the cold out'. Such phrases arise out of mental images of something real and hostile out there.

As for evil, even if it were truly an 'absence of goodness', we can never feel satisfied describing it as such; it just doesn't sound right. Think, for example, of the Nazis exterminating six million Jews in the Second World War. A mere 'absence of goodness'? Surely not. We have to accept that evil is real, and that in turn means someone – and I am suggesting the finger points to you and me – is to blame for it.

A Shadow Side to God?

But is that fair? Are we being too hard on ourselves? There are alternatives.

Earlier, I said how God made it possible for evil to enter into the world; he had no choice. In order that we might be able to turn to him in love, he had to give us free will. It is our misuse of that freedom that leads us into creating the evil. God is not to be blamed for that; he remains wholly good.

But suppose he is not. Suppose we have been wrong in assuming God to be wholly good. Like the rest of us, he might be a mixture of good and evil. This was the view of the Swiss psychologist Carl Jung. He claimed that there might be a dark side to God; he called it the shadow.

I have a great respect for Jung and much of what he had to say; he was himself a deeply religious man. But when it comes to his suggestion that God himself was partly evil – that it was God who created the evil in the world as well as the good – that part I think he got wrong for several reasons.

First, I believe I meet up with God in my prayer life. The idea that the kind of God I meet is to some extent evil simply does not ring true. He just isn't like that. Second, I believe that Jesus was such a special person that it is likely he was indeed the Son of God. And when we look at the kind of person Jesus was, it is hard to imagine that he could have lived a perfect life if his heavenly Father had not also been perfect.

No, trying to shift the blame for evil onto God is no way out; it is a vain attempt to let ourselves off the hook. And indeed Jung himself, in other writings, came closer to the truth in my view when he maintained, 'We need more understanding of human nature, because the only real danger that exists is man himself... We know nothing of man, far too little. His psyche should be studied because we are the origin of all coming evil.'

The Devil

Of course, in all this we are assuming there is just the one God. Another way of dealing with evil and other awkward facts of life, is to have more than one God. The Greeks and Romans, for example, believed there were several gods, each in charge of some aspect of life: Mars the god of war, Venus the goddess of love, Bacchus the god of wine and so on. So why not say the God we worship is wholly good; but there are other divine beings too. The Bible itself speaks of the devil – a fallen angel. It could be the devil who is at fault.

Today most people regard the devil as something of a joke: red cloak, horns and tail, and armed with a trident. But are we right to be so dismissive? Joseph Conrad held that 'A belief in a supernatural source of evil is not necessary; men alone are quite capable of every wickedness.' That might be so. But surely it is only when we think of evil as somehow personified, a conscious force tempting us to go astray, that we begin to treat it with the seriousness it deserves. Even if the devil did not exist, it could still prove useful to retain a mental image of an evil personage trying to lead us astray.

Evil is something that humans do – it is the sum total of the bad thoughts and actions of conscious human beings. So evil is personal. Perhaps the word 'devil' should stand for all that is evil in our own minds. As the character Ivan says in Dostoevsky's *The Brothers Karamazov*, 'I think if the devil does not exist, but man has created him, he has created him in his own image and likeness.'

Whether the devil exists as a person in his own right, beyond what is to be found in our own minds, is perhaps neither here nor there. Even if we believe the devil to be real, we are still left with the thought that it was God who made the devil along with all the other angels. So attributing the blame for evil to the devil, still does not get us far.

Evil as a Necessity

Earlier, I mentioned how some people dismiss evil as an 'absence of goodness'. I said how I didn't like that suggestion. But looking at evil in that way does draw our attention to a close connection between good and evil. According to that earlier idea, 'evil' was defined in terms of goodness (the absence of goodness). We had to already know what the word 'goodness' meant in order to understand what the word 'evil' meant. That remains true. Without goodness we would not know what evil is and vice versa – without evil, we would not know what goodness was.

It is an odd thing about words that they gain their meaning to some extent from their opposites. Take the word 'yellow'. When objects are lit by a yellow sodium street light, they all appear to be yellow – different shades of yellow, but all yellow. Suppose we had been brought up imprisoned all our life in a closed building where the only light came from such lamps; suppose also that we had never seen what the world outside was like. Although we had been lit all our lives by yellow light, would we know what the word 'yellow' meant? No. In practice, we understand the meaning of the word 'yellow' because we live in a world where objects are normally lit by white rather than yellow light, making some objects appear yellow and others not (they might be blue or red). We say, 'This one is yellow; that one is not.' It is only by being aware of examples of things that are not described by the word, as well as things that are, that one can understand what that word means.

In the same way, we understand what the word 'goodness' means only by being familiar with its opposite: the word 'evil'. A world in which there was no evil would be a world in which there would be no goodness either. Evil is the price that has to be paid for goodness.

When is Something Evil and When Not?

Another thing to bear in mind is that it is not always clear whether something is evil or not. Take the nuclear bomb. With its capacity to eliminate all life on the planet, it is widely regarded as the world's greatest evil. We cannot escape the shadow of fear it casts. There was a time when the bomb had a particular relevance for me. I had just gained my doctorate from university, in nuclear science. One of the options open to me was to get a job developing nuclear weapons; that was what some of my friends went on to do. I decided not to; I felt uneasy at the thought of spending the whole of my life making bombs, which either would never be used, or worse still, might be used.

So does that mean the nuclear bomb is pure evil? No. The reason for having the bomb is to deter other people from attacking you and using their bomb if they have one. The explosions at Hiroshima and Nagasaki brought the Second World War to a sudden end. The loss of life in those cities was tragic. But it is surely the case that those two bombs halted the war, and in doing so, saved countless other lives, which would otherwise have been lost had the war been allowed to run its natural course. Not only that, in the years that have passed since that war, there have been numerous occasions when feelings ran so high between nations that they came to the very brink of starting the third world war. What stopped them? Fear of the nuclear bomb. There can be little doubt that many are alive today thanks to the nuclear bomb. That being so, it is hard to regard the bomb as purely evil. For that reason, while continuing to believe that declining the offers made to me to join the nuclear weapons industry was the right decision for me, I have never in any way condemned my fellow students who decided otherwise. We might wish that scientists had never invented the bomb in the first place, but they did, and there is no going back on that now. We have to live with it and deal with it wisely.

The bomb is one way in which scientists have made life more complicated for us all. Some people think that science as a whole is evil. It certainly has a lot to answer for. We do not need reminding that as a direct result of science and technology, we are faced with many problems: global warming, the destruction of the ozone layer, pollution, cloning, genetically modified crops and so on. But this is to overlook the many good things that come from science, medical science in particular. It is easy to forget that only a few hundred years ago, one had a less than fifty-fifty chance of surviving into one's teens. So it is unfair to dwell solely on the 'evils' of science and ignore the good side.

And what is true of science is true of so much of life. It is not always easy to label certain things as 'good' and others as 'evil'. Perhaps there is some truth in the assertion of British philosopher Samuel Alexander: 'Evil is not... wholly evil; it is misplaced good.'

A Continuous Spectrum Between Good and Evil

Another reason why the distinction between good and evil might not be as clear-cut as generally supposed is that there can be a continuous gradation from one to the other.

For example, take something that is clearly wicked: the Holocaust. The officers in charge of exterminating Jews in the death camps sought afterwards to exonerate themselves on the grounds that they were merely carrying out orders; they were performing their duty; they were conforming to the will of the state. Doubtless they were also thinking of their career advancement, as would any father and husband responsible for the well-being of their own families. To perform their task they had to develop a sense of detachment; they could no longer allow themselves to imagine what it would be like to be placed in their victim's position.

This ability to adopt a detached attitude towards one's fellow human beings was at the heart of their evil acts.

But now let us consider something not so extreme. The Holocaust was brought to a close by the ending of the Second World War. In order to win that military victory, the men and women of the Allied forces were trained to be detached from what they were doing. A bombardier can only press the button to release his bomb load if his mind is concentrated on the factory or the bridge he is trying to blow up, and not on the people, the human beings just like himself, who are also down there. Is it wrong for armed forces to cultivate such detachment, even when such forces are to fight in a good cause? Pacifists would say yes, others no.

So let us move still further along the spectrum of detachment. You are the head of a firm that is running into difficulties. The only solution is to 'downsize', as they euphemistically call it. Unless some of the employees are sacked, the firm will go bankrupt and everyone will be out of a job. It is your responsibility as boss to decide who is for the chop. Such a decision cannot be made without developing a sense of detachment; you simply cannot allow yourself to think too much about the inevitable economic hardship your decision will cause to the unlucky ones and their families. Is such a decision evil? Hardly.

Or, finally one might consider a mother having to remove the sticking plaster from the cut finger of her child. She knows the action will cause momentary pain and crying, but the plaster needs to come off to be replaced by a fresh one. Once again, a measure of detachment from the suffering of the other person is required.

With this last example, there could be no doubt that the mother's action is solely for the good of the child. But where along the way did detachment from the feelings of the other shade between being evil and being good?

Do Evil People Know They Are Being Evil?

Closely related to this blending of good and evil is the question of whether the person committing the evil actually knows that what they are doing is wrong. Take the Muslim extremists who flew airplanes into the World Trade Center buildings on that fateful day, 11 September 2001. To us, what they did was an unspeakable evil. But did they themselves see their action in that light?

From the way they died invoking the name of Allah, it would appear not. Perhaps it would have been impossible for anyone to perform such an act if they were consciously aware of the evil of it. As far as they were concerned, they were engaged in a struggle against the evils of Western capitalism – the relentless erosion of their own culture by the customs and values of a superpower. To some extent we can share that concern. One doesn't have to be a terrorist to see the downside of globalization. There is nothing inherently wrong in expressing legitimate fears about the growing dominance of multinational corporations and trying to restrain their excesses. Such was the soil in which Islamic terrorism took root, and which was to be the justification for what they eventually did. It was a cause they believed in.

That being the case, were they to blame for what they did? How can we take to task someone who did not know their action was wrong? That, after all, is the standard defence put forward on behalf of accused persons who it is claimed have diminished responsibility; they are mentally incapable of judging right from wrong.

I do not see that such a defence holds in the case of those terrorists. They might not have known at the time that they were doing wrong, but that is because of all that had gone on before: their willingness to go along with years of training and indoctrination regarding the methods permissible for bringing about their desired ends. It is their cooperation in the progressive corruption of their character that renders them blameworthy. We are all personally responsible for our character, the kind of person we allow ourselves to become. A corrupt character leads to evil acts, and the performance of evil acts contributes to the further corruption of the character.

But what of the voice of conscience? Does God not speak to all of us directly through that moral sense within? We need to be careful here. God indeed may speak to us in that way, but the so-called voice of conscience is not to be equated with God's voice itself. Conscience is a channel through which God can speak, but only if we allow him. If we habitually ignore the promptings of conscience, it becomes blunted and ineffectual; the voice is stilled, and God can no longer get through to us in that manner. All of us need to take care that we do not permit our sensitivities to be gradually eroded over the course of time. If we are not vigilant, who knows what we might one day become capable of doing?

Naturally Good People?

I have said that we humans are to blame for evil, and this comes about when we turn our backs on God and his ways. But that raises the question of why God made us the way he did: a people that was likely to reject him. Couldn't he have made us differently? Suppose we had been made such that no one ever wanted to turn their back on God. Could we not have been given free will so that it was possible for us to reject God, but in practice no one ever did? In other words, why not have a world in which people just naturally loved God and were good?

By way of an answer, suppose a hypnotist puts a young woman into a trance and says, 'When you wake up, you will find that you are in love with me. One, two, three – wake up.' Sure enough, the subject wakes up and declares that she is madly in love with the hypnotist. Would that love be *real* love?

Although it could be argued that the subject had been given nothing more than a suggestion – a hypnotic suggestion – so that she might have gone against it, the hypnotist presumably would not be all that happy if that was the only kind of 'love' he could expect. It would certainly not be a love he would value as much as that of someone who, of their complete free choice, chose to love him. The fact that there has been pressure applied, even of a subtle kind that merely tends to make the person love him, would still downgrade the value of that so-called love.

Naturally Bad People?

Indeed, if anything, God seems to have gone to the opposite extreme and made us with a tendency to depart from his ways and be evil, rather than the reverse.

According to the theory of evolution, we humans are evolved animals. That being so, we can learn something about ourselves from the study of other animals. What we find is that the behaviour of other animals is largely governed by their genetic make-up; it is instinctive, meaning they act in certain ways without having to think about it. They inherit these behaviour patterns from their ancestors. So for example, my pet cat, Curry, will instinctively stalk and kill a bird. This she does even though she might already be full of cat food and unable to eat another mouthful. She can't help herself; it is the way she is made. It is the kind of behaviour her ancestors had, behaviour that helped them to find food and survive under conditions very different from those in which Curry finds herself today. Long ago, if a cat did not have this killer instinct written into its genetic code, it stood less chance of surviving and so producing descendants of its own. That's why the only cats you get today are the descendants of the 'killer-type' cat. And that in turn is why Curry behaves the way she does today, even though there is no longer any need for her to do so in order to survive.

Being evolved animals ourselves, it is only natural to expect that we too would have inherited certain behaviour patterns from our ancestors. This would be the type of behaviour that in the past would have helped towards the survival of those ancestors, and so would, in the main, be selfish and self-centred. And that is how we come to have a built-in tendency towards such behaviour today – the sort of behaviour that, taken to extremes, becomes evil. This seems to have something to do with one of the messages to be gained from the Adam and Eve story in the Bible. There we read how Adam and Eve gave in to temptation to eat the fruit of the forbidden tree. They had no need of it, there were plenty of other things to eat, but they just decided to go along with their natural desires to take whatever they fancied, even though it did not belong to them.

The name 'Adam' means 'man'. The story is not simply about a particular person and his wife;

it is saying that *all* humans have a built-in tendency to behave in this self-centred way, a tendency God expects us consciously to resist. Today's modern theory of evolution seems to be saying much the same kind of thing about our basic human nature.

Altruism

However, I don't want to overdo this idea of selfishness – the idea that because we are evolved animals, we are invariably selfish. That is not the case. There are circumstances where our genetic make-up orientates us towards acting unselfishly, or altruistically.

Take, for example, the way a mother will sacrifice herself for her children. In the animal kingdom, there are mother birds who sacrifice their lives for their young. When a predator approaches, she will leave the nest where her young are and make a great display in order to attract attention towards herself and away from the nest, even at the cost of her own life. It is an instinctive behaviour pattern, one that is all to do with survival. Survival? How can that be? She is committing suicide! It is certainly true that she, as an individual, has increased her chances of dying, but the important thing here is not the future of the individual; what counts is the survival of a piece of genetic coding – a code that makes her behave in that way. The mother is not the only one possessing the genetic coding; her young have it too; they inherited it from her. As far as the survival of the coding is concerned, it is more advantageous for it to live on in the young rather than in the mother. In a sense, the mother is dispensable; she has done her job of passing on the code to the next generation. A coding that prompts a mother to sacrifice herself for her young, should the need arise, has an enhanced survival value over some other, which might say, in effect, 'Always look after yourself.'

So that is one form of altruism we expect to arise out of evolution: animals, including humans, will be prepared to sacrifice themselves on behalf of close relatives, those who share with them in large measure the same coding.

Biologists speak of a second form of altruism: 'reciprocal altruism'. This is where animals help each other out, but only on condition that they too get something out of the arrangement. Thus we find one monkey grooming another monkey, getting out the nits from its fur in places the first monkey finds hard to reach. This is done on the understanding that the first monkey will do the same in return – that it will reciprocate. Being helpful to each other like this is in the interests of both. That sort of behaviour is also to be found in humans. We have a phrase for it: 'You scratch my back, and I'll scratch yours.'

Strictly speaking it is not altruism at all. True altruism is where the individual puts him or herself out for someone else, even when there is no chance of being paid back. For example, if you give money to Oxfam, which is then passed on to the starving people of Ethiopia or elsewhere, there is no way such people are ever likely to repay you. They are not closely related to you, so acts of kindness like this cannot be put down to examples of the first type of altruism. Dag Hammarskjöld expressed the view, 'Perhaps a great love is never returned.' Indeed, there is the love for those who have harmed you. 'Perfect love means to love the one through whom one became unhappy,' as Søren Kierkegaard put it. Such genuine acts of altruism are very hard to account for in terms of some piece of genetic coding that has arisen out of our ancestors' struggle for survival.

No, it would seem to me that the process of evolution will give rise to creatures who mostly – not always, but mostly – will be inclined towards selfish and self-centred behaviour.

The Myth of Childhood Innocence

This has never been a popular idea. When cooing over a newborn baby, it is hard to resist the thought that the baby we are looking at is basically good, sweet and innocent. If, in later life, it ends up as a football hooligan, blame the parents, or bad influences at school, or TV violence, or poor living conditions. The baby's innocence has become corrupted from outside. The answer? Change society, create decent living conditions, teach children the difference between right and wrong, set them good examples, show them love and kindness. That way the innocence they started out with will be preserved and allowed to flourish.

Sounds good. The trouble is it doesn't work out like that. I am not saying that one should not improve the conditions in which youngsters are brought up and educate them as to right and wrong. But even with an excellent upbringing, some will still go astray. Each day, countless parents wring their hands in despair asking, 'Where did we go wrong?' More often than not, they did not go wrong. They weren't perfect parents (no one is) but that's not to say they didn't do a fairly decent job. No, the reason children do not always turn out as one would wish, is that they are individuals who to a large extent decide for themselves what kind of person they will be. They make their own decisions as to how much they will resist their inborn tendency to behave selfishly, and to what extent they will simply go along with it.

An Alternative to Evolution?

Which all sounds pretty depressing. Here we are, evolved animals with a basic tendency to put our own interests first, instinctively competing with each other, making exceptions only in respect of close family members, or if cooperation means there is something in it for us. These behaviour characteristics, though no longer essential for survival, are integral to our make-up. Indeed, given the awesome power of modern-day weapons, such aggressive tendencies put the long-term survival of the entire human race in jeopardy. This is the legacy of our human evolutionary history, and there is no escaping it. Not only are we a danger to ourselves, these inherited traits make it very, very difficult to lead the sort of good, loving, kind, self-sacrificing lives that God is supposed to want of us.

Did it *have* to be evolution? Earlier, we saw that there would have been problems with God making us like robots, pre-programmed to be good and loving; there were even doubts about the genuineness of any love we could have shown towards God had we been put into some kind of hypnotized trance where we were irresistibly inclined to 'love'. But it does seem as though God has gone out of his way to make things especially hard for us. Was there no alternative way of bringing us into being, which would not have required us to develop such strong tendencies towards selfishness and aggression towards others?

One problem is that the very complexity of the human personality entails our various defining characteristics being interlinked. While we might from a moral standpoint condemn our selfishness and aggression and wish to be free of them, we would not want to lose those other qualities commonly regarded as the reverse side of the same coin, such as ambition and drive, characteristics essential to the attainment of distinctively human goals. As the French writer Anatole France put it, 'Every vice you destroy has a corresponding virtue, which perishes along with it.'

I don't pretend to know the answer as to why

God chose evolution. But perhaps it has something to do with this: God needed to create us in such a way that we could offer him genuine love. That being so, it was out of the question for him to construct each one of us, atom by atom, according to some detailed blueprint of his own design. Why? Because if that creature had later turned out to 'love' God, it could be argued that this was simply because God had built that behaviour in; it was all there in the original design; it's the 'robot problem' once more. No, in order for the love to be real, there has to be some distance between God and his creature.

Of course, if there had been a second Creator, there would have been no problem. But there wasn't; there was only the one Creator God. So with God being ultimately responsible for all creation, how could he produce a creature that possessed in some measure a degree of independence from him? There had to be something in the nature of the creature that God did not specifically design into it. The creature had to some extent to be free to make itself.

Evolution seems to have been the answer. It goes like this:

Offspring, in the main, resemble their parents (colour of skin and hair, height, intelligence and so on). These characteristics are encoded in one's genes – the offspring's genes being based on those of the parents. In the main, the offspring receive faithful copies of the genetic codes of their parents. But from time to time, there are mistakes in the copying process, random mistakes. These give rise to new codes producing new physical features and behaviour patterns that were not present before. Some of these new characteristics might give the individual a competitive edge when it comes to finding food or avoiding being killed by predators. The new characteristic might be the ability to run exceptionally fast, or the possession of a particularly sharp set of claws, or a tougher than average protective hide. Whatever the characteristic, individuals fortunate enough to possess it will have a greater chance of surviving to an age when they can mate and have offspring of their own, and those offspring inherit the new beneficial characteristic. Other individuals not endowed with that characteristic will have less chance of surviving to the point where they have offspring, and hence less opportunity of passing on their less beneficial characteristics.

What this means is that members of the next generation, on average, will benefit from having the new, improved characteristic. The new characteristic is being selected out, in a natural kind of way. Hence 'evolution by natural selection'. Beneficial characteristics that help the individual to survive better tend to be preserved in later generations; the less helpful characteristics die out. That way, ever more complex creatures develop, better and better adapted to surviving in their surroundings.

Ultimately, this process led to humans, our most important distinguishing characteristic being our intelligence. Our final form depended a lot on chance, pure chance. If the slate were to be wiped clean, and the evolution process restarted, it is most unlikely that it would be we humans who emerged second time round. Intelligent creatures, yes, but they would not look like us or have many of our features; the random events that produced them would not have been the same as those that produced us. In saying this, I do not mean God had to stand by, keeping his fingers crossed, hoping something interesting would develop. God knows everything, including the future. He knows it is going to work out all right in the end. One way or another, creatures will emerge capable of relating to him.

Evolution might be seen as God's way of getting round the problem of how he could put some distance between himself and us; to some extent, chance had a hand in shaping us. Having in this manner gained a certain independence from God, we have the opportunity of genuinely choosing whether or not to love him.

Could God have adopted some alternative to evolution? We shall probably never know. All we do know is that, for better or worse, we are the products of evolution, with all that entails when it comes to us possessing self-centred instincts.

The Image of God

Not that it is all gloom and doom. We have this tendency to be sinful and selfish, but it also says in the Bible that we are 'made in the image of God'. What does that mean? It means that we have it in us to rise above our natural failings. Just because we have an inborn tendency to be self-centred rather than God-centred doesn't mean we have to give in to it, we can fight it; we can choose to do otherwise.

As we have seen, religious believers have to struggle with the problem of evil: why there is evil if God is good. But unbelievers also have a problem – the problem of goodness: why there is goodness if there is no good God. The source of evil can be traced back to our inborn tendency to put our own selfish interests first; but where are we to look for the source of the goodness we sometimes display? Earlier, I pointed out that sometimes we behave in a genuinely altruistic manner, at some cost to ourselves, and with no hope of being paid back later. It is hard to see how that kind of altruism could have had 'survival value' and become encoded in our genes. And yet despite that, we do, from time to time, show that sort of behaviour.

Religious people, like myself, believe that God has somehow managed to put his own stamp on us. Deep down we are drawn towards him and want to be like him. This results in a constant battle between, on the one hand, our natural tendency to behave in a self-centred way, and on the other, the longing search for a more fulfilling goal. It is this battle that makes it so special to be human.

The Fall

I am sometimes asked about the part of the Adam and Eve story that describes them as starting out in a state of perfection – paradise. It was only after they ate the forbidden fruit that sin entered and everything got spoiled. We call this the Fall. How are we to understand the Fall in the light of what we have been saying about evolution?

The scientific picture of our origins does not in any way back up the idea that things were perfect to begin with. But that is not to say the Bible got it entirely wrong. As life forms evolved and became more complex, there came a point where, for the first time, one of our distant ancestors began to take an interest in more than where to find shelter, food and sex; it began to reflect on the meaning of life, and on whether it might have a purpose. It began to wonder how it ought to behave in the pursuit of some higher goal. This is where the first glimmerings of a sense of right and wrong put in an appearance. Our ancestor had to decide whether to continue always doing things by instinct, or whether sometimes there might be reason to take some other course of action. From now on it could make a conscious decision not to obey its natural instincts; it had a choice. And that in turn meant that, for the first time, an individual could be held responsible for his or her actions.

And that is where sin came in. Up to that point the world was sinless, as the Bible says. This was not because everything was perfect (it certainly wasn't), but because until then the word 'sin' had no meaning, just as it has no meaning if you try to apply it to one of today's animals. I can't talk of my pet cat, Curry, as being 'sinful' or 'evil' when she kills a bird; she knows no better; she has no alternative but to follow blindly the dictates of her instincts. No, it was not that things were perfect to start with and only later became spoiled. Rather, it was the case that to begin with there was nothing that could rightly be spoken of as sinful. Evil entered into the world only when our ancestors began to make genuine choices as to how they would behave.

But Do We Really Have Free Will?

All of this assumes we actually do have a choice, that we really are free to decide what course of action we shall take. But are we?

It is certainly hard to see how free will arises. We know that what happens in our mind is closely related to what is going on in the brain, its chemical changes and its flows of electricity. But these processes are thought to take place according to strict physical laws. This seems to be telling us that, given enough information about what is going on in the brain at any moment in time, we ought in principle to be able to apply the laws of nature and work out what will happen next. What is more, this will apply even when the person whose head we are examining is 'making a choice'. It will seem to her that she is making a choice that could go either way, depending on what she decides to do. But with our extra knowledge of the working of her brain, we would see that 'the decision' went the way it did because that was the only way it could go. Knowing the state of her brain before 'the decision', we could work out, ahead of time, what it would be after 'the decision' was made, in other words we could work out what her choice was going to be even before she knew it herself.

So is the idea that we have free will merely self-delusion? This is a big, big problem. In an attempt to answer it, some people appeal to quantum physics. When dealing with very small objects, like the subatomic particles taking part in chemical processes and in flowing electrical currents, one has to be careful. These tiny particles do not behave like the big particles we are used to in everyday life: lumps of rock, or snooker balls. They do not obey the laws of nature we were taught at school. Instead, they obey a totally different set of laws known as 'quantum physics'. In the strange world of the very small, one *cannot* predict what is going to happen next, at least not with certainty. If one sets up exactly the same situation twice, it is unlikely the result will turn out the same as it was the first time round. For example, shoot one electron at another, in exactly the same way as one did before, and it will bounce off at a different angle. There is no way of determining ahead of time which angle it will be. All one can do in advance is work out the chances of it being different angles: perhaps a 40 per cent chance of being in one angular range, a 32 per cent chance of another, a 13 per cent chance it will end up somewhere else and so on. And there is no way of getting round this element of uncertainty. It has even been given a name: the 'Uncertainty Principle'.

What this means is that we were wrong when earlier we pictured ourselves examining someone's brain and being able to work out exactly what she would be doing and thinking next. This cannot be done; the best we can do is place our bets as to what *might* happen, and then leave it to chance.

So is that the answer to the problem of how we come to have free will? The behaviour of the brain is not fixed in advance at all, so neither are the mental thinking processes that accompany those brain processes. This would seem to open things up a bit and allow some freedom, just what we need if we are to make our own choices. That is indeed what some people think.

But I am not so sure that this is the answer. Quantum physics shows that knowing what the brain is doing at one point in time does not allow us to predict what it will do next. However, what we have put in place of this certainty is chance. Now, I don't see how 'making a conscious decision' is the same thing as 'leaving things to chance'. When one tosses a coin to decide an issue, one is leaving it to chance *as distinct from* making a conscious decision.

There is an alternative approach to the problem. The brain, though made of subatomic particles, is a very special arrangement of subatomic particles: it is *conscious*. It is conscious in a way that a couple of particles banging into each other are not (at least I presume they are not). That being so, perhaps consciousness is responsible for something new going on in the brain, some new type of behaviour, which goes far beyond that expected of the individual subatomic particles from which the brain is made.

What do I mean by something 'new'? Well, just as physical processes in the brain affect what goes on in the mind, perhaps it also works the other way round: what goes on in the conscious mind affects what happens in the brain. In other words, we think of the mind as a thing in its own right, capable of affecting the physical body, interfering if necessary in its normal running.

This might even be done in a way that, strictly speaking, does not violate any law of nature and is impossible to detect. We have already seen that we cannot predict for certain what will happen next; we can only give the odds of several possible outcomes. Well, what if the conscious mind interfered with the odds? What if it changed the chances of what happens next in such a way as to ensure that what it wants to happen will indeed happen? Anyone examining the brain at the time might think, 'Oh, that wasn't very likely,' but they would not be able to say that it was against the laws of nature, the quantum laws allowing a wide range of possibilities.

The idea of the mind and the brain

interacting with each other is not as popular these days as it once was. Most people today think that the mind and brain are so closely related to each other, so interdependent, that it just doesn't seem right to treat them as distinct, separate things that push each other around, with or without the apparent freedom offered by quantum uncertainty.

So what is the answer to how we come to have free will? I simply do not know. Perhaps, when all is said and done, we are mistaken in claiming we have free will, or at least, we are not as free as we would like to think ourselves to be. One thing is certain, however: we shall never be able to dispense with the idea of free will. There is no escaping the need to make decisions; it is all part and parcel of living one's daily life. And this would be true even if we were to convince ourselves that there was no need to make any 'decisions', either because all our future actions were set in concrete anyway, or because they were to be governed purely by quantum chance. A decision not to make further 'decisions' because such decisions would be unnecessary – what will be will be – is in itself a decision! And subsequent decisions not to alter that original decision would also be decisions.

So even though we do not understand how, from the physical point of view, we could be free, it does not alter the fact that we still have to live our lives as though we are free. Life would not make sense otherwise. We have to take responsibility for our actions. A criminal cannot stand in the dock and tell the judge, 'It was not my fault, guv; it was just the laws of nature doing their stuff on me. I had no choice but to go along with it all.'

Free will is a practical reality, even though we have no satisfactory way of understanding intellectually how we come to have it. For all practical purposes, we are in charge of our life, we stand on our own two feet, we deserve the credit when we do a good job and, yes, we are prepared to take the blame when things turn out to be a mess. The final word on this I leave to Samuel Johnson: 'Sir, we *know* our will is free, and *there's* an end on't.'

An All-Powerful God

I said at the start that God was all-powerful. But, you might be thinking, if we humans bring evil into God's world, and evil is not what God wants, doesn't that mean God can't be all-powerful? Surely an all-powerful God could get whatever he wants.

It depends what we mean by 'all-powerful'. Even if someone is all-powerful, that doesn't mean they can make a square triangle. A square triangle is impossible, and even all-powerful beings cannot be expected to do the impossible. Perhaps there is something 'impossible' about the idea of a world in which love exists, but evil does not. As we have seen, if we are to show God genuine love, we have to have been given the freedom to make up our own minds about it, and if we are free, it follows that we can misuse that freedom.

Again, God is not all-powerful in the sense that he has delegated some of his power to us; he allows us to share in his power. This we see in the way he lets us run our own lives. He trusts us to get on with things and make lots of decisions without his interfering with us all the time. So God's power is limited in this sense too – but only because he chose to limit his power in this way.

This is not to say that he has lost control. He is not a God who has to keep his fingers crossed, hoping everything will work out all right. If God knows the future, he knows that, in the end, all will be well. There will be setbacks along the way; it might appear from time to time that evil has won the day. We might feel that things are going so badly wrong, God ought to step in and put a stop to at least the worst excesses of evil. But, like it or not, that is not God's way. God's power is not a controlling power.

There can be different kinds of power: throwing thunderbolts is one; the power of life and death wielded by a despotic ruler over his citizens might be another. But there are more subtle kinds of power: that of the editor of a newspaper influencing public opinion; that of an inspiring teacher; or that of a parent gently reasoning with a child instead of commanding obedience 'because I tell you'. God's power, I believe, is one of persuasion.

Religion Itself as a Source of Evil?

Evil arises, as I have said, through our turning away from God. From that you must not think that I am claiming that atheists are bad, while religious people are good. Human beings are more complex than that. There's good and bad in all of us. Mind you, I also reject the view, often put to me by atheists, that religion has caused more harm than good. 'More people have been killed in religious wars than any other way.' The number of times I have heard *that*!

Such a claim is simply not true. Although religious people can be drawn into waging war like anyone else, it is rare for religion itself to be the cause of the war. Take Northern Ireland, for example. The two sides of the conflict have been given religious labels – 'Protestants' versus 'Catholics'. Protestants and Catholics do differ in their religious beliefs on a number of points: prayers to the Virgin Mary; the sense in which the communion bread and wine become the 'body and blood of Jesus'; whether the Pope is infallible in his official pronouncements; and so on. But it would be absurd to think that these differences played any part in the thinking of the IRA or loyalist terrorists as they planted their bombs.

The two world wars were not caused by religious differences. And that even goes for the killing of Jews by the Nazis. The Nazis did not commit those terrible crimes because the Jews would not convert to Christianity. Their motives were racial hatred and envy of the success of Jews in business and other walks of life – motives that would still have been there even if there had been no religious differences.

What of those Muslim extremists of 11 September 2001? As we earlier noted, they believed they were waging 'a holy war' against the USA. They had been taught that as a result of their action, they themselves and seventy of their relatives would go to heaven, and as a further reward, they would have the pick of seventy-two heavenly virgins. I recall reading a newspaper article at the time in which a well-known atheist vehemently attacked religion, declaring that such brainwashing was what 'religion was all about'.

It was an absurd thing to say. The vast majority of Muslims made it clear at the time that they were as revolted by this act as anyone else. Islamic religious leaders throughout the world, even those known to be highly critical of America, were quick to condemn the actions of the fanatics, and to offer their sympathy to those who had lost loved ones. They pointed out that true Muslims followed the teaching of the Prophet Muhammad as laid down in the Qur'an. There the Prophet says 'God has made inviolable for you each other's blood and each other's property.' He goes on to declare that to destroy the life of one individual amounts to destroying the entire human race, and that those who disturb the peace of society and spread fear and disorder deserve the severest punishment. That is what true religion is about; it is as true for Islam as it is for Christianity.

The trouble is that religion, like any other human activity, is capable of being twisted and distorted into something evil by a fringe minority. It is as foolish to claim that religion is all about brainwashing people into committing wicked acts as it is to claim that everyone going to football matches is a knife-wielding hooligan out to make trouble, and that this is what football is all about.

Which is not to say that evil acts done in the name of religion are solely the work of crazed, warped minorities. Sometimes church leaders themselves are guilty. Take, for instance, the Inquisition. The Church has always tried to pass on what were judged to be correct teachings concerning God. Individuals expressing contrary views were branded heretics. Naturally enough, church leaders disapproved of the spread of views that, in their opinion, had already been tested and found to be false. The Inquisition was set up to help stop the spread of these misleading ideas, which was fair enough. The trouble was the way they went about it. The Inquisition thought nothing of torturing heretics and burning them at the stake. Indeed, in later years it was not just heretics who suffered. Those accused of being possessed by the devil – witches – were also burnt at the stake. It was all quite shameful. No one today would dream of defending such actions.

As I said, fanatics are to be found not only on the outer fringes of religion, but occasionally right at the centre of the Church itself.

A World Without Religion

Given that religion can stir up such strong and, at times, dangerous feelings when not channelled properly, it is not altogether surprising that some are inclined to the view that the world would be a better place without religion altogether. This, however, ignores all the good that has come from religion. Not only that, the experiment of doing away with religion has already been tried – with horrific results.

Take the Soviet Union under the communist rule of Joseph Stalin. Stalin made a determined effort to stamp out religion once and for all. Churches were closed; religious believers were hunted down and persecuted without mercy. At school, youngsters had it rammed into them that religion was nothing but out-of-date, ignorant, superstitious mumbo-jumbo. The plan was that once the older generation had died out and been replaced by those who had been brought up in this atheistic way, religion would have withered away and become a thing of the past. What then? Well, obviously the world would be a better place with everyone being able to live peaceful lives free from the old conflicts stirred up by religion. An atheist's paradise.

Except it did not work out that way. By the

time Stalin died, he had killed 20 million of his own people. Nor was this an isolated experiment in doing away with religion. China suffered an even worse fate. At the last count, it is thought that communist Chairman Mao was responsible for the death of some 60 million of his fellow citizens. And, of course, history is littered with the deeds of those for whom religion meant nothing: Hitler comes immediately to mind. Such people stand as vivid reminders of just how wicked humans can be when their instincts are no longer held in check by a religious set of values.

So what do I conclude? I am saying that I fully accept that many evil acts have been done, and continue to be done, in the name of religion. They are shameful and there is no excuse for them. I and my fellow religious believers are embarrassed by them. Not only do we disown them, but we are sure God disowns them too. The Bible quotes Jesus as saying, 'Not everyone who says to me "Lord, Lord", will enter the kingdom of heaven, but only those who do the will of my Father in heaven.' I reckon a lot of so-called religious people are in for a shock on the Day of Judgment! But to go to the other extreme and try to do away with religion is to jump out of the frying pan into the fire. Trying to go it alone without the help of God, only makes our chances of doing evil that much greater.

Fortunately, there is more to us than just the basic instincts we have inherited from our ancestors – those instincts that, if not kept in check, lead to selfishness and evil. We are also imprinted with a deep yearning to seek after God. The communist attempt to stamp out religion in the Soviet Union, lasting seventy years, turned out in the end to be a complete failure. The authorities simply could not root out that deep yearning. Since the end of communist rule there, religion has made a remarkable recovery – to the extent that, in 1999, the award ceremony for the Templeton Prize for Progress in Religion was held in the Kremlin – which had until that time been the very heart of the communist government.

Opposing Evil

That is really as much as I want to say about the nature of evil and its origins. But one thing we have not touched upon: what ought we to *do* about evil? A very practical question.

Edmund Burke, the Irish-born British statesman and philosopher, once said 'It is necessary only for the good to do nothing, for evil to triumph.' Take the Second World War. Adolf Hitler was bent on invading other countries. British prime minister Neville Chamberlain tried to reason with him; he thought he had persuaded Hitler to change his mind. They signed an agreement. But Hitler had no intention of keeping his word. The German army invaded Poland and went on to conquer many other countries as well.

What do you do about someone like Hitler? You cannot negotiate or reason with him. If you are weak, he will simply take advantage of you. So do you just sit back, do nothing and hope for the best?

Pacifism

Some people say that is exactly what we should do. We ought not to oppose force with force – evil with evil. Two wrongs don't make a right. Jesus instructed his followers that if they were struck on the cheek, they should 'offer the other cheek also'. If necessary, you should allow people to walk all over you. This is done in the hope that your opponents will eventually see the error of their ways and will be won over by your loving, peaceful example. Such is the view of the pacifist.

I admire the pacifists I have met, and I respect the stand they take. Does that mean I go along with them that the Allies should have laid down their arms and not resisted the advance of Hitler's forces? Is that the only course of action open to Christians?

It is a tough question. There is no easy answer. To see how difficult it can become, consider this: if the Germans had been allowed to invade Britain, I along with everyone else would have suffered hardships of one kind or another. Fair enough, one might think, just grit your teeth and get on with it. But what of my Jewish friends? What do I say to them? How about, 'Sorry to hear that when the Nazis get here they will round up your family, imprison you all in a concentration camp and gas you to death. Fortunately, I'll be OK myself, not being Jewish. I only wish I could do something to try and save you. But I'm afraid I can't; it is against my religious principles to resist by using force. But I will pray for you.'

Of course, it is difficult to be sure how one would really react in a situation like that. But somehow I can't see myself saying anything of the sort. Assuming I was brave enough, I would not stand by and do nothing; I would take up arms to defend my Jewish friends. And I can think of many situations where I would find it hard – indeed impossible – to adopt a pacifist stance.

A Just War

Indeed, pacifists are very much in the minority. Most Christians are prepared to take an active part in war, given sufficient reason to do so. Because we believe there are times when evil people should not be allowed to have their way unopposed, there has arisen the idea of a 'just war'. Clearly, before embarking on such a course of action, all peaceful options must first have been tried and found to be ineffectual. It must be in a good cause – fighting for freedom and all the other things we believe in. Also, one must use no more than the minimum force needed to halt the evil that would otherwise be done. Unlike Neville Chamberlain, Winston Churchill when he took over as prime minister, had no doubts that the German invasion had to be opposed by force; it was the only kind of language a dictator like Hitler would understand. As far as Britain and its allies were concerned, the Second World War was a just war.

The trouble is that, when embarking on war – even a 'just war' – one steps onto a slippery slope. What does 'reasonable force' mean? It is hard to tell. Constant exposure to the violence of war blunts one's sensitivities. What at one time would have been regarded as shocking, later no longer seems as repugnant. The level of violence tends to increase with time. So it was that as the war dragged on year after year, dreadful things were done on both sides. 'When one has given Evil a lodging, it no longer demands that one believes it,' said Franz Kafka. Our bombing of innocent women and children in Dresden was just as horrific as anything the Nazi bombers had done. War leaves everyone soiled and guilty.

And yet, I believe it was right to fight that war. I do not see how we had any alternative but to oppose force with force. And the successful outcome of that conflict – the fact that we and other nations live now in freedom and relative peace – appears to be the justification for that course of action.

Jesus as the Model

But you might say that is all very well. You are a Christian, and as such, you should model your life on that of Jesus. Are you saying that you can imagine Jesus taking part in a just war? Can you see Jesus ever taking up a gun and deliberately killing someone with it?

I have to confess my answer to that is no. I cannot imagine him doing any such thing. Jesus' teaching that we should love our enemies, rather than hate them, keeps coming back to me. I suppose it is that which convinces pacifists that they are right and I am wrong. Frankly, I do not know what my answer to this is. One half of me admits the logic that if Jesus would never kill anyone or resist force with force, then I as a loyal follower of his should do the same. I recall, for example, how Jesus did not defend himself when he was wrongly accused; he just allowed himself to be crucified. And it probably is the Christian thing not to defend oneself.

But then I think back to that imaginary conversation with my Jewish friend where the point was not whether I should defend myself (my life not being in any particular danger) but whether I should stand by and do nothing to defend my friend who, being Jewish, would certainly be put to death through my lack of action. Had Jesus been a non-Jew like me, what would he have done in that situation? Would *he* have stood by and done nothing? Probably not. Which is not to say he would have taken up arms. I reckon he would have said something along the lines, 'I cannot defend you, but at least I can die with you.' I reckon that, even if he had been born a Gentile, he would have passed himself off as a Jew and got himself sent to the concentration camp – along with those Jewish friends. That's just a wild guess. But at least it would be in line with the sort of thing he actually did do in his earthly life. He allowed himself to be sacrificed for others. He died the death of a common criminal even though he was not himself a criminal.

If that's what I suspect Jesus would have done, ought that not be my course of action? Were another Hitler to arise, ought I to be a pacifist, choosing to die alongside my Jewish friends – rather than taking up arms to wage war in their defence? I suspect the answer is yes. But having said that, I cannot actually see myself doing it. Does that mean I am not a very good Christian? Probably. I simply don't know.

Part of the trouble is that we are not very good at taking the long-term view. When we act, we are not looking very far into the future. We see what is directly in front of us, and we tend to react automatically – like taking up arms to defend one's friends and loved ones. It seems the natural, obvious thing to do. Jesus took the longer view. Jesus, when faced by the power of the Roman governor and the chief priests, did not oppose them; he allowed himself to be killed. Those witnessing his crucifixion were convinced that his cause was now lost. But it wasn't. Two thousand years on, Christianity is still here; it is the Roman empire that has vanished. So whose strategy prevailed in the end?

Punishing Crime

We have talked about wars – 'just' or otherwise. But what about the evil encountered in normal everyday life. Every society has to deal with the problem of crime – petty crimes like shoplifting, all the way up to murder. What are we to do about criminals?

The answer seems to be to punish them, through making them pay fines, sending them to prison, and in some countries executing them for serious crimes like murder. Part of the reason is undoubtedly revenge. But mostly it is to do with deterring crime. By punishing the criminal, one hopes he or she will learn a lesson and think twice before committing further offences. One hopes further that not only the criminal, but anyone else who might otherwise be toying with the idea of taking to a life of crime might also be persuaded to think again.

I visited Beijing in China some years ago. I was struck by how safe the streets were. There was hardly any crime. Why? You only had to watch the TV broadcasts to see the reason. Time and again one saw on the news criminals being led through the streets publicly to be executed – and for quite trivial things. To judge from that, it would seem we ought to introduce more severe punishments here – stiffer prison sentences, flogging – and bring back hanging for murderers at least. Indeed, there are people who call for tougher punishments like that; to them it seems sound common sense.

Except that it is not that simple. People sent to prison are thrown together with other prisoners, some of whom have spent much of their life in prison and are experienced in criminal ways. Young first-time offenders can come under the influence of these hardened 'old lags'. Far from coming out of prison reformed and ready to take their place in society, youngsters can emerge knowing how to be better criminals! Indeed, a large number of them soon find themselves back in prison again for some new offence.

As for bringing back the death penalty for murder, time and time again it has been shown that the death penalty has no effect at all on the rate at which murders are committed. Don't ask me why that should be so; I don't understand it. But it is true. Perhaps it is simply the case that when someone is in the mood to kill another person, the last thing they are thinking of at the time is what will become of them if they get caught.

The Role of Forgiveness

What we do know is that evil gives rise to more evil. Just look at what is happening in the Middle East. One killing leads to another. You kill one of our people, and we will pay you back by killing one of yours. That killing in turn leads to another. Because no one remembers who started it all, the tit-for-tat goes on and on.

There has to be another way. Martin Luther King once said, 'Jesus eloquently affirmed from the cross a higher law. He knew that the old eye-for-an-eye philosophy would leave everyone blind. He did not seek to overcome evil with evil. He overcame evil with good.' In place of revenge, there has to be forgiveness. Not that it comes easily; no one pretends it is easy to forgive someone who has wronged you – particularly when that person hasn't even asked for your forgiveness because they are not sorry for what they have done. But forgiveness is the only way to break the chain of violence.

One also has to get to the source of the evil. We have to understand why the person acted in the way they did. Are they feeling angry about something, and if so, do they have good reason for feeling like that? It is only when one gets to the source, when one discovers the real motives at work, that there is any chance of putting the situation right.

Goodness Out of Evil

The other thing we have to bear in mind is that, although evil is likely to lead to more evil, sometimes it does not; goodness can be born out of an evil situation. What starts out as pure evil can sometimes be used to accomplish some good; the power of evil can be deflected. It might take a long time; there might be a lot of pain to go through first. But in the end good can come from evil.

Take, for example, 11 September 2001. People around the world, including many who would not normally see themselves as friends of the USA, were united in offering sympathy and goodwill. Perhaps it needed something as horrific as that to awaken us all to the terrible depths to which we humans can sometimes sink, and to the need for us all to join in a common cause to defeat the evils of terrorism.

PART 2

Why Suffering?

Let us now turn to the question of suffering. It is clearly linked to the problem of evil. As we have already noted, evil results from people misusing their God-given free will – a freedom we must have in order for there to be love. The term 'evil' means deliberate acts leading to harm, injury and suffering. So a world in which love is the guiding principle has to incorporate not only evil, but also the suffering that results from the evil. Suffering becomes part of the price to be paid for love.

But that in itself will not do. While a lot of suffering does indeed arise out of the deliberate, evil actions of people, that does not by any means account for all suffering. What of that caused by natural disasters: earthquakes, famine and floods? What of the innumerable other ways we are liable to fall foul of nature: diseases, accidents and so forth? Suffering arising from such causes cannot be laid at the door of human evil.

A Punishment for Sin?

Or can it? A persistent idea throughout human history has been the notion that suffering must be a punishment for sin. God is a God of justice, so those who suffer most must have sinned the most. It appears an obvious way of making sense of why some people suffer more than others.

To some extent there might be an element of truth in this. Some suffering does appear to be self-inflicted. If one deliberately drives a car recklessly and gets injured in a crash, then one surely cannot escape a measure of blame. The same is true if one starts playing around with drugs, or drinking to excess and gets hooked on the habit, or if one indulges in unprotected promiscuous sex and contracts Aids, or one is seduced by the beauty and sunshine of California to the extent of discounting the earthquake risk of living in that region. We do have to take responsibility for our actions. But mostly this is not the kind of suffering we have in mind. And in any case, the fact that one might from time to time bring suffering upon oneself does not necessarily mean that it is a punishment from God; it is a simple case of cause-and-effect arising from one's own decision to act in a certain way.

The suggestion that suffering – *all* suffering – is a punishment from God is explored by the Bible in the book of Job. Job, we are told at the beginning, was a good man; he was blameless. He was rich and had a large family. Everything was going well for him. But then disaster struck. He was robbed, his servants murdered, all his sons and daughters perished when the house they were in collapsed during a hurricane. Furthermore, he contracted a dreadful disease that covered his entire body in painful sores. His friends (so-called) told him that all of this must have come about because he had been especially wicked; God was punishing him for it. Job would have none of it. He wasn't perfect, but he wasn't *that* bad.

That was a story from the Old Testament. Much later, in the time of Jesus, the idea of suffering being a punishment for bad deeds was still very much around. We call to mind the story in John's Gospel, chapter 9, of the man born blind. 'Who sinned, this man or his parents?' asked Jesus' disciples. 'Neither this man nor his parents,' was the reply and, as if to underline what he had said, Jesus promptly cured the man 'so that the work of God might be displayed'. Jesus clearly distanced himself from the view that suffering was a punishment for sin. And in our own times, it is manifestly clear when we look around at the people we know, that those who suffer most are no more wicked than the rest of us.

Hindus have a different approach. They believe in rebirth; one keeps coming back to this earthly life. At each incarnation, one is born into a way of life that reflects how one has lived previous lives. All the misfortunes that befall one are the inevitable and just outcome of what one has done in previous lives; the responsibility is entirely one's own. It is undoubtedly a neat solution, but that is not how Christians see the situation. In the absence of supposed misdoings in some previous life, they cannot explain away suffering as a deserved punishment.

A God of Neglect?

If God is not actively punishing people, perhaps he simply does not care what happens to us. Having created the world, he has left it to get along without him; he is indifferent to us – neither interested in what we do, nor in what becomes of us. He is a God of neglect.

Either that, or God is more interested in the global picture rather than the detail. The living world is to be regarded as a painting. You and I are but individual brush strokes helping to make up the whole. To appreciate a painting the viewer has to stand back and take in its totality. If one peers too closely, with one's nose up against the canvas, all one sees is swirling, confusing, messy brush strokes. Moreover, the overall harmony of the painting might require some of these strokes to be black. Thus, so this cold and rather heartless explanation goes, we should not be surprised to find that certain individuals have to live messy, dark lives. It is all for the good of the whole.

Again this is not the Christian view. As we have said, God is a God of love. He is very much concerned about us – and furthermore, us as individuals, rather than as a part of collective humanity. Love is what the world is all about. Christians go so far as to believe that he was so concerned about us, he sent his Son to share in human existence alongside us.

God Didn't Know What He Was Doing?

Which brings us to another possibility. Though it is assumed God is all-wise and all-knowing, what if he isn't? Suppose the world is a terrible mistake; he did not anticipate how things would turn out. Doesn't it say in the Bible how he was sorry he had

made us, and that is why he sent Noah's flood?
If he hadn't anticipated how badly humans would
behave, perhaps he also hadn't worked out all the
unfortunate natural disasters that would arise out
of the kind of world he was making.

Although there are people, including several
respected theologians, who hold that God is no
more capable of knowing the future than we are,
that is not the orthodox view. The traditional
understanding of God is that he knows the future;
he has foreknowledge. That being so, he would
know that the world he was making would lead
not only to many people rejecting him, but also
to many innocent people having to suffer. And
yet he did nothing to stop it.

God is Powerless to Stop Suffering?

But *could* God have stopped it? Perhaps he has
known all along there would be much suffering,
and this is something he very much regrets. But
he is powerless to do anything about it; he has
to stand aside helplessly while it all happens.

Such a view would appear, on the face of it, to
go against the traditional understanding of God as
being all-powerful – omnipotent. Except, of course,
where God's 'power' is concerned, we must be
careful. We have talked before about God's power.
Recall how even an all-powerful God cannot do
logically impossible things. We have already noted
that God could not create conditions where genuine
love could take root without giving us our freedom.

Could there not have been some additional restraint upon him – some further condition that had to be observed for his overall objectives to be achieved in the long run? What form could such a restraint take?

The Need for a Neutral Environment

If we are to have free will, and we have seen the need for that, then it has to be exercised in an environment that is predictable. Each of us must be able to anticipate what the likely outcome will be of any course of action we might choose to take. That means the environment must be law-like – it must obey set rules. It must be a *neutral* environment – one that can be used for good or ill.

Not only that, it must be a common medium – one through which we can interact with other individuals. We make ourselves known to other people through the physical world. Our physical bodies operate in the physical world. It is a world that cannot bend its rules to meet the passing whim of any particular individual. That might infringe the interests of some other person – one who has just as much, or as little, right as ourselves to have things their own way. We might want it to rain so as to save us the trouble of having to water our garden; someone else might want fine weather because they are going on holiday. You can't please everyone.

So the arena in which we operate has to be fair – fair to everyone – the world we all jointly inhabit has to have a nature of its own. And that is how we find the world.

But having said that, it follows that the blind, automatic working out of those laws of nature will from time to time lead to some unfortunate consequences. It is bound to happen. It is one of the prices we have to pay for our freedom. It is a logical requirement, and even an all-powerful God cannot circumvent that requirement.

But, one might ask, would it not have been possible for God to have devised a world run on somewhat different lines, a world that was still reliable enough for us to exercise free will with anticipated consequences, but one that was not afflicted by the bad, harmful side-effects such as volcanoes, earthquakes and diseases like cancer? It is hard to say. I can only presume it wasn't.

A God Who Intervenes?

In that case, why not a world that was largely predictable, but when some unforeseen bad consequence was about to occur, God would step in and personally interfere with the smooth running of the laws of nature. In other words, why not a world where each case of suffering from natural causes was circumvented by a one-off miracle? After all, an all-powerful God could supposedly suspend the laws that he himself had originally put into operation, should he so wish.

There are, of course, many reported cases of God answering prayer in this manner. Nor does one have to rely on anecdotal evidence. There is an increasing number of investigations carried out along more-or-less scientific lines where teams of intercessors pray for one group of hospital patients and not for another. The patients, all suffering from the same condition, are divided up in this way so that the latter group acts as a control. It allows a direct comparison between those who are prayed for and those who are not. Most of the studies carried out to date appear to show a positive correlation between prayer and increased chances of good recovery. These results, in view of their statistical nature, need to be treated with caution. As in all such studies, there can be disagreement as to whether the results are statistically significant. But if these early indications are eventually confirmed, they would be consistent with a God who does indeed intervene on occasion in response to petitions.

That is as may be. What we can affirm is that, regardless of what one personally thinks of such studies, and the efficacy of intercessory prayer in general, such instances of God's direct intervention are likely to remain the exception rather than the rule. For most intents and purposes, we are to assume that nature will follow its normal course.

Suffering as an Opportunity

But why? If God is prepared to step in and help on certain occasions, why not others? Why are some people miraculously healed and others die in agony? Were the intercessors not praying hard enough? Is God arbitrary in his mercy?

Such questions are only to be expected. When faced with someone who is suffering, it is only natural for us to think that the relief of that suffering should come first. But clearly God does not always see it like that. God appears to have other priorities: our spiritual development, culminating in life eternal. Perhaps on occasion a measure of suffering has an integral part to play in the achievement of those long-term goals. Perhaps we need to recognize that suffering does not have to be regarded as necessarily and exclusively evil.

If God made a habit of stepping into the breach whenever he was asked, this could not but erode our own sense of responsibility in regard to caring for those in need. Having asked God to intervene on behalf of the patient, there would be nothing left for us to do but sit back and let God take control.

'So what?' one might ask. As far as the recovery of the patient is concerned, that might be a good thing; God is likely to make a better job of it than us. Maybe. But there would also be a serious downside. It would jeopardize the extent to which we would be able to demonstrate our own love for each other. After all, how do we normally demonstrate our love for others? By having good times together? Lots of sex and partying? Such activities might indeed be part of that relationship. But they do not in themselves constitute proof of love. They are enjoyable activities in themselves; we might be engaging in them merely for our own self-gratification, nothing to do with genuine love for the other. No, love is demonstrated through the way we are prepared to put ourselves out in attending to the needs of others.

One sees this in little things: a mother getting up in the middle of the night, even though she is desperately tired, in order to feed and change the nappy of the baby. Or one might find it in big things: a husband devoting himself to the care of his housebound wife suffering from the ravages of multiple sclerosis, rather than going off with another woman. Or one might find it in the way someone gives a big donation to a charity seeking to relieve the miseries of refugees or victims of famine. This is a demonstration of love for those one has not even seen personally.

The extent to which we are prepared to sacrifice our own interests on behalf of another – in other words, the extent to which we are prepared voluntarily to undertake a measure of suffering or hardship ourselves to alleviate that of another – is the only reliable proof of our love for them. That being so, to have God repeatedly stepping into the breach to make all things well by miraculous intervention would nullify these opportunities for us to demonstrate our own love for each other.

Suffering can bring people together, even

those who do not particularly get on well with each other. 'Think, when you are enraged at anyone, what would probably become of your sentiments should he die during the dispute,' said English poet William Shenstone. Suffering compels sympathy; through it we recognize a shared humanity. As the apostle Paul says, we 'weep with those who weep'.

And it is not just a matter of feeling more emotionally compassionate towards the victims of suffering. People are drawn together as they work in the common cause of relieving suffering: helping out at the local hospital or hospice; raising money for Oxfam or Christian Aid; prison visiting; getting in shopping for the housebound; joining a prayer group; and so on. All these activities forge links between people, and they all arise out of the existence of suffering.

Not that suffering is a Good Thing. I am not saying that. The relief of suffering is undoubtedly a laudable aim and an end always to be pursued. But that does not alter the fact that the existence of suffering can be marshalled for good; it provides unparalleled opportunities for demonstrating love and concern for others. A great deal of good can come from how we respond to the needs of those who suffer.

Strength from Suffering

Then there is the effect suffering can have upon the sufferers themselves. Sometimes, in the face of calamity, a person will abandon their faith in God. The suffering they have to endure proves to be too much for them; it comes between them and God. Suffering can have that alienating effect; it can cause despair, disillusionment and a sense of futility and meaninglessness.

But often it is not so. Setbacks and difficulties can lead to a strengthening of ties with God. Through suffering, it is possible to come to a deeper realization of our dependence on God, and through surviving the calamity, a deeper appreciation of his ultimate protection. It can also lead to a deeper appreciation of one's own inner strength in the face of adversity. 'How sickness enlarges the dimensions of a man's self to himself,' observed Charles Lamb.

The closest brush with death I myself ever had was when I fell off a cliff while on holiday in Switzerland. I landed flat on my back on a boulder, cracking ribs and compacting vertebrae in the spine. Having been stretchered off to hospital by the Mountain Rescue Team, I was confined to bed for many weeks. During that time, I could not help reliving the accident over and over again. I kept thinking of how I could so easily have rotated through a different angle during the fall and hit that rock head first – with fatal results. What a narrow escape! I recall how, from my hospital bed, I could see a tree outside the window. The sun was playing on the leaves. For hours, I contemplated that tree. It was as though I was seeing a tree for the first time. I had never seen anything so beautiful. Thirty years ago this happened, but in my mind's eye I still see that tree; I still experience that profound sense of gratitude to God for my preservation and for all the wonderful, beautiful things of life.

Perhaps you have had an equivalent experience. Many do. There we are, wrapped up in our daily activities and the pursuit of our goals and ambitions, coping with life on a day-to-day basis, failing to get things in perspective, not seeing the bigger picture, not appreciating and savouring life. Then it happens; some disaster, some shock. We are brought up short, jolted out of our routine. And often this is through suffering. Many a life has been changed – for the good – by a long, enforced spell in hospital, or a brush with death. As C.S. Lewis put it, 'God whispers to us in our pleasures, speaks in our conscience, but shouts in our pains – it is his megaphone to rouse a deaf world.' This is often the case provided, of course, the pain is not unbearably intense and unremitting.

If things go well, we are inclined to be complacent; it is human nature. It is so much harder to attend to one's devotions when there is nothing to worry about. It is in times of trouble we are driven to our knees in prayer. Too many people think of God in the same way as an airman regards his parachute, something to be called on in emergencies. If that be the case, if that is the only way God can jolt us out of our stupified self-satisfaction, so be it; let there be emergencies.

Indeed, we ourselves might not be the ones

to suffer. When are we most inclined to offer God thanks for such benefits as our sight, hearing and mobility? It is when we meet up with people who are blind, or deaf, or confined to a wheelchair.

Transformation

The emergence of something good, beautiful and positive from what was originally ugly and painful can be seen in the example set by the newly opened Imperial War Museum North in Manchester. No one relishes the idea of confronting the horrors of war. But the experience offered by this museum is altogether different. The building is an absolute stunner. The architect, Daniel Libeskind, has taken the image of a globe shattered by war and reassembled three of the fragments. One of the shards swerves downwards close to the canal side and represents war on the sea; a second heaves and buckles to symbolize war on land; and the third and most spectacular soars and curves heavenwards, a reminder of aerial combat. All the jagged profiles and surfaces of this extraordinary structure are clad in gleaming aluminium.

The interior is equally breathtaking, with walls, ceilings and corridors assaulting the visitor with acute jutting angles, creating a sense of vulnerability, which was just how it felt during the war. Everything about the building is deeply symbolic of war. Even the site on which it is built was once a savagely bombed industrial complex manufacturing engines for Spitfires and Lancaster bombers. And yet all that ugliness, suffering and evil has been transfigured into a thing of great beauty, something to uplift the spirit.

One finds the same kind of thing happening within the Christian religion. Anything more horrific and shameful than the crucifixion of Jesus is hard to imagine. And yet, over the course of time, that rough-hewn, ugly, blood-stained wooden cross – the Roman equivalent of the gallows or the electric chair – even that has been transformed. Millions of people today wear a cross of gold, or silver, or precious stones. It symbolizes their faith, a constant reminder of the sacrifice of Jesus, but also now a thing of beauty.

And what goes for the ugliness of war, and the pain and suffering of Jesus, can also apply to the very worst that we ourselves are called upon to endure: mourning the loss of a loved one, coming to terms with untreatable cancer, picking up the pieces after a broken relationship, or whatever. Humans have this remarkable ability to take the very worst and make something of it. Everything that is most beautiful and noble and admirable about the human soul arises out of suffering. As George Eliot put it, 'Deep, unspeakable suffering may well be called a baptism, a regeneration, the initiation into a new state.'

I suppose what I am saying is this: suffering cannot be written off simplistically as an unmitigated 'evil'. In itself, it need be neither good nor evil. It is how we use it that counts. It is that which determines whether it remains evil, or is alternatively transformed to become good.

The Function of Pain

And what is true of suffering in general is certainly true of that aspect of suffering: physical pain. The sensation of pain is not something totally bad. In some respects, it is undoubtedly a good thing, a vital part of our ability as evolved animals to live and survive in an environment that can sometimes be hostile. Pain is a warning of danger and injury. The pain of placing a hand on a hot object is a warning to withdraw the hand to avoid being burnt. It needs to be unpleasant so as to make the avoidance of danger immediate and instinctive. Internal pain, like that of appendicitis, is likewise a warning that something is wrong inside us and needs attention.

The function of pain is to teach us how to operate successfully in our environment. The prolonged headache we get when we bang our head on an overhanging tree branch provides us with an unpleasant memory that encourages us in future to take greater care to avoid such injurious encounters. The prolongation of the pain is not needed to tell us that we have hit our head – we know that by now – no, it is teaching us a lesson about our future actions.

As I say, pain can be a good thing. But of course, there are aspects of pain that cannot be accounted for so easily. Arthritic pain, for example.

It does not arise from something injurious that one did. There are no lessons to be learned from it as regards what future action one should take. What good comes from the suffering and pain of childbirth? Indeed, so much of the suffering in the world seems unnecessary.

These sorts of pain serve no useful function, except that the person suffering from it is able to set an example to others facing adversity. Which brings us back to the question of what one does with one's pain. Human suffering can ennoble the individual, or destroy that person. Through suffering, one can either become a better person – or a bitter person.

It is rather like a clay pot being put into the potter's kiln to be fired. Unless it is subjected to extreme heat it will remain soft clay, no use to anyone. It has to pass the test of fire before it becomes transformed into pottery, useful pottery. Of course, not all clay pots survive the test. If it has a flaw in it, a trapped air bubble say, it is likely to explode and be destroyed in the process. It is through the trials and tribulations of suffering that we develop our spiritual souls. And just as every piece of pottery that has ever been fired is still around today in some form or other, so our souls when fired in the kiln of suffering become immortal.

Jesus employs a different image – that of the vine being pruned. Just as the gardener prunes the vine to make it more fruitful, so God prunes every fruitful branch 'so that it will be even more fruitful'. And that pruning involves suffering.

This is a far from comfortable picture of God.

Some would say it portrays him as hard and stern. They are troubled as to why God should adopt such a line, rather than taking better care of us, ensuring that we are safely protected from all possible harm.

My thoughts go back to my cat. Like most pet owners, I care for her in a particular kind of way. I try to make sure she never comes to harm, never wants for anything. That is what being a good pet owner is all about. But that is not how God is with us. We are not his pets. He has something more challenging in mind for us. He wants us to be strong, to stand on our own two feet, to take responsibility for our own destiny, and to some extent be independent of him. This is so that we can, of our own choosing, respond to him in a loving relationship. It cannot be a relationship between equals, of course, but certainly something much richer than the dependence of a pet on its owner.

In order to acquire this distinctive individuality, we must expect to go through some tough times and suffer some knocks. There will be circumstances when God stands back and allows us to take a few steps on our own, in much the same manner as a mother will at some stage allow her children to walk to school on their own, despite the obvious hazards encountered along the way in terms of dangerous roads needing to be crossed. The fearful child might at first feel abandoned; the mother appears to be less caring than she ought. But in truth, she is acting out of the long-term good of the child. In the same way, God forces upon us a measure of independence, he lets us face hazards, all for our ultimate good. He is not being any the less loving for it.

In any event, God does not stand to one side allowing us to get on with things wholly on our own. We have been encouraged to pray to him, and indeed, to ask him for what we need. That is why, for example, we pray for the sick. Not that those we pray for always recover in the way we would like. God is the only one who knows the full circumstances. In his infinite wisdom, he might realize that the long-term greater well-being of the person is better served in some other way than by responding to our request with a straight yes. But I'm convinced that he does always hear our prayers and acts on them. God's response might result in an amazing cure, which none of the doctors thought possible. Such things do happen. On other occasions, help might come through being given the strength to live through the bad times, the ability to come to terms with the inevitable. God has many responses to prayer ranging from a straight 'yes', through 'yes, but not yet', or 'yes, but not in that way', through to a straight 'no'. God always hears and gives an answer, an answer best suited to our longer-term betterment.

God's Involvement

That is one way God is anything but detached from our predicament. There is another. If one is a Christian, then one believes that God, far from merely offering encouragement from the sidelines, or being content to answer prayers at a distance, did himself enter into the created world in human form as Jesus Christ. As a result of that full and active participation, he was to experience suffering directly, and to a degree most of us are unlikely to be called upon to endure. Though God does not prevent us from suffering, he does the next best thing: he comes and shares in the suffering with us. In so doing, God has encountered suffering, not only physical but mental also, even to the extent that Jesus was to experience on the cross the ultimate desolation of feeling abandoned by God.

The suffering and death through crucifixion of Jesus was seen at the time as the greatest possible evil, nothing less than the killing of the Son of God. But even this was to be transformed. Indeed, it has become the greatest good. We feel much closer to God as a result of what he did for us. Some might even go so far as to agree with the French poet Paul Valéry, when he declared 'Christ's death has impressed the world more than his resurrection.'

I would not myself subscribe to that view. The cross shows that God is prepared to suffer with us, but more importantly, the resurrection of Christ proclaims that ultimately God has conquered sin, suffering and death.

Suffering in Animals

So far we have talked only of human suffering. In that context, it is possible to see how some ultimate good can arise in the form of a closer walk with God. But what about the suffering endured by animals? We can hardly say that such suffering is there so that the animals can demonstrate their love for each other and for God.

There seems to be so much suffering in the animal kingdom. It is integral to the whole process of evolution by natural selection. Evolution by natural selection is a process that we tend to regard as the story of the glorious ascent of humankind. We would, wouldn't we! But what of all the individual animals and species that had to be wiped out over the past 3,000 million years in order for us to make that ascent? Whereas most humans die because their body wears out or they succumb to disease, vast numbers of animals are killed by other animals. 'Nature red in tooth and claw', as Tennyson put it. Why did God choose such a seemingly cruel way of bringing humans and modern-day animals into existence?

In the first place, we must be careful not to project on to animals that which is distinctively human. We assume they suffer pain. But do they, and if so, to what extent? If we cannot get into the mind of another person and experience their mental sensations, we are even less likely to be able to understand the experiences of animals. For example, does a worm experience pain when it is cut in two? It writhes about as though it were in agony, but both halves are doing that. Are we to understand that both halves are in pain? Does the worm now have two minds where there used to be only the one? Or is there no mind at all, no sensation of pain? Does a fish experience pain when the angler's hook gets stuck into the roof of its mouth? Presumably the angler thinks it doesn't. And that is probably the majority verdict or there would be an outcry against the infliction of needless pain on an animal simply for the pleasure of the angler.

Moreover, we know that the degree of pain we humans suffer depends to a large extent on how much attention we pay to the injury. It is not uncommon for a footballer to leave the field of play at the end of the game and be surprised to discover that he has sustained a gash to his leg. Casting his mind back he might be dimly aware of a particularly fierce tackle he sustained, one that was probably the cause of the injury. But at the time he had thought nothing of it, his mind being wholly concentrated on getting the ball. In other words, the pain felt at the time was almost non-existent because his attention was distracted. Suggest to him that one should now deliberately kick him in the other leg (to even things up, perhaps) and his reaction will be quite different. This time he would indeed feel the pain, because his mind would be on it. As the French essayist Michel de Montaigne observed, 'A man who fears suffering is already suffering from what he fears.' And we see the same kind of thing at work when people are put under hypnotic suggestion or subjected to acupuncture; both can reduce the pain sensation.

The reason I am saying this is to make the point that if mental attention is an integral feature of humans feeling pain, it might be argued that animals, having less overall mental capacity than ourselves, might feel less pain because of that lesser capacity.

Now, you might feel, with some justification, that this sort of argument lets us off the hook too easily (to say nothing of the angler). In any case, when it comes to the more developed creatures, such as cats, dogs, monkeys and our close relatives, chimps and gorillas, the assumption must surely be that they do feel pain, and significantly so. But even in such cases, we must keep things in perspective. Though such animals might more often than not suffer a painful death as the result of an attack by a predator, at least it is over pretty quickly. For most of their life, they have probably had a reasonably comfortable existence – sleeping, lying out in the sun, having sex and eating animals they have themselves preyed upon. A painful but mercifully short death might not be so big a price to pay.

Generally speaking, mental suffering is accounted worse than the physical suffering arising from pain. It can hardly be doubted that, compared to animals, humans have the greater capacity for mental suffering. Voltaire declared, 'Animals are to be envied. They know nothing of future evils.' They may to some extent experience fear, anxiety, frustration, and they may mourn the loss of a loved one, but feel remorse, shame, failure, guilt, depression? I shouldn't think so, at least, not significantly. As for the anticipation of one's ultimate death, its awful finality and its significance for the overall meaning and purpose of life, I doubt such a prospect poses much of a problem for animals. In short, I do not see animals as having the capacity to suffer the mental agonies we sometimes endure. There is little evidence of animals voluntarily ending their lives because life has become unbearable for them. In contrast, more humans commit suicide because they can no longer put up with their mental trials than are driven to that unhappy end by physical suffering.

The Degree of Suffering

Returning to the question of human suffering, it might be argued that it is all very well claiming there has to be suffering in order for there to be a demonstration of love, but why so much suffering? 'We humans are such limited creatures – how is it that there are so few limits when it comes to human suffering?' asked the French writer Pierre Marivaux.

In a sense, God *has* set limits. As Victor Hugo said, 'Beyond a certain pitch of suffering, men are overcome by a kind of ghostly indifference.' Under great pain and torture, the victim is at some stage likely to pass out, to become unconscious. Then there is the limit set by death. The sufferings of this mortal life will come to an end when we pass to the life beyond. We suffer, yes; but only for a time.

Speaking of death as a way out of suffering, if life is so full of misery and suffering, as some claim it to be, why don't more people bring it to a premature close; why do they not commit suicide? The means are readily to hand: an overdose of sleeping tablets, no pain, no trouble, go to sleep, and that's it, problem solved. And yet few take that way out. On the contrary, we hang on for dear life. What is that telling us about the balance between joy and suffering?

There are exceptions, of course. There are those who are so weighed down by their troubles that they do go ahead and commit suicide; there are others for whom the compensations of being artificially kept alive are so minimal, they plead for their life support system to be turned off. But this is not the experience of most. In the life of the average person, suffering is more than outweighed by life's other compensations.

All suffering is relative. A small child, on falling and grazing his knee, yells and screams. To hear the cries one would think it was the end of the world. And indeed, for the child, that is indeed how it seems; he has nothing else to compare it with; he has never experienced anything so alarming. It is only later in adulthood, when visited with greater pains, that the severity of a grazed knee is viewed from a different perspective. If somehow the intensity of human suffering were to be scaled down – in response to our protests that at present it is excessive – our sense of what constitutes 'severe' suffering would quickly readjust. Who can doubt that, even on the new reduced scale, we would still end up convinced that its higher levels were extreme.

In this connection, I should perhaps point out that there is a school of thought that holds that even the worse forms of suffering and evil are to be regarded as trivial; they are not worth arguing about. The so-called problem of evil and suffering has arisen merely because we have got things out of proportion. According to this 'solution' to the problem, all that counts is the world of the spirit; everything happening in the material world, including suffering, is of no importance.

I doubt many will find consolation in that. Far from human suffering being trivial, one of the things we have to come to terms with is that, where God is concerned, he never does anything by halves. This is so whether we are thinking of the vast scale of the universe (who ordered all that?), or the aeons of time that had to pass before intelligent life put in an appearance. It is the same with suffering. This is not a toy world; it is not a playschool, pretend-type of world; it is the real grown-up, genuine article. If a little self-inflicted sacrifice and suffering is a small indication of love, then nothing short of deep suffering is needed as a sign of deep love.

There are two kinds of evil: the sort that leads to suffering and another that leads to triviality. Human beings are such wonderfully complex creatures, capable of great depth and spirituality. But this largely passes us by. St Augustine once wrote, 'men go out and gaze in astonishment at high mountains, the large waves of the sea, the broad reaches of rivers, the ocean that encircles the world, or the stars in their courses.

But they pay no attention to themselves.' Many coast through life at a superficial level, never exploring their potential. This is a waste of life, and as such it is evil. As Thomas Carlyle declared, 'The tragedy of life is not so much what men suffer, but rather what they miss.' Sometimes a measure of suffering is the only way to explore this potential and hence avoid the greater evil of a trivial, misspent, wasted life. Certainly it is the case that only a life lived with intensity can yield great love.

I suppose this has something to do with the way we are prepared to take on certain risks in order to enjoy a more fulfilled life. You can't ski without running the risk of breaking your leg; you can't ride a bike without the risk of crashing; you can't climb a mountain without the risk of a fall; you can't enter a competition without the risk of losing. These risks are something we voluntarily take on in order to add zest to life.

What I am saying is that all of life is like that. You cannot have the pleasures of sight without running the risk of the loss of your eyes; you cannot have the sense of touch without the risk of pain. And you certainly cannot enjoy all that goes with a loving relationship without exposing yourself to the risk of rejection. A rich life is a costly, painful life.

A Price Worth Paying?

The idea of God choosing love as the prime purpose of his creation – as opposed to happiness –

was a far from obvious move. In the light of what necessarily follows from that choice, in terms of evil and suffering, one might be tempted to doubt the wisdom of God's decision. To put it bluntly, is love all it's cracked up to be?

Take love between humans. There are certainly many advantages to living alone. You can have your house or flat just the way you want it; eat what you want, go out and do whatever you want, when you want to do it.

But that is not what most people settle for. Instead they prefer, if possible, to be involved in a loving relationship with someone else, even though that entails self-sacrifice, compromise, many difficulties and conflicts of interest. It is a price most of us are prepared to pay. Even having gone through all the upheaval and trauma associated with divorce, people are still liable to seek out a new partner with whom to share their life.

We can but conclude that there is something about a loving relationship that is more rewarding than a life lived alone; it is something worth suffering for.

God and ET

In calling attention to the supreme position held by love in the world, I would not want to give the impression that I was advocating that the universe was created simply for God to enter into a loving relationship with us humans here on planet earth. That naturally enough was the assumption in biblical times, given that no one then knew anything about other planets capable of supporting life. But with our modern-day scientific observation of the many planetary systems out there in the cosmos, I would think it most unlikely were the earth to be uniquely the home of intelligent life. I expect the universe to be teeming with life forms at least as intelligent as us, and in some cases, surpassing us. Having reached a level of intelligence comparable to our own, I am sure such life forms will be equally capable of entering into a loving relationship with their Maker. I suspect that all the issues we have been discussing in terms of the necessity of evil and of suffering will be as relevant for them as they are for us.

The World for its Own Sake

Not only do I believe that God is as much interested in extraterrestrial life forms as he is in us, I suspect God also takes delight in the universe as a creation in its own right, quite apart from its utilitarian function as a home for life. If we mere mortals can be struck by a sense of awe and beauty when gazing at the heavens, and take delight in a sunset or a towering snow-capped mountain range, why cannot God?

Natural disasters only appear evil when seen from our own perspective as creatures living in that world. They will not necessarily appear so to God. On the contrary, they are but the natural outworkings of the laws of nature – the beautiful laws of nature; it is creation doing its thing, and as such, is good. We must not think that the sole purpose of creation is to bring into being intelligent creatures like ourselves and that, as a consequence, everything must be geared to our requirements and our convenience. For 12,000 million years – most of the vast history of the universe – there was no intelligent life at all. But I am sure God enjoyed the world then, and that he will continue to enjoy it long after life on earth and on other planets has ceased. God respects the integrity of the running of his physical creation for its own sake, regardless of the fact that this inevitably gives rise to occasional unfortunate consequences for life during its brief transitory sojourn in the universe.

The Practical Response to Suffering

In this chapter, we have been taking a look at some of the intellectual arguments that have been voiced around the problem of suffering. One thing is certain, a reader of this book who happens to be going through a particularly difficult time at present will have gained little comfort from the arguments. That was not a realistic expectation. In fact, from the very outset, I probably ought to have sounded a warning note that the purpose behind this book has nothing to do with offering consoling thoughts for those currently facing some crisis in their lives: the loss of a loved one, coming to terms with a terminal disease, coping with non-stop pain, picking up the pieces of one's life after divorce, and so on.

During such periods of one's life, the very last thing one wants is for someone to start arguing the case for why such suffering is only to be expected. 'Nothing is more depressing than consolations based on the necessity of evil... It is ridiculous to try to alleviate misfortune by observing that we are born to be miserable,' the French philosopher Montesquieu warned. There is a time and a place for everything. Rational argument certainly has a part to play in putting together a faith founded on intellectual integrity. But it is an exercise to be engaged in only when life is on a more-or-less even keel as far as one's own personal suffering is concerned. Such arguments require a certain level of detachment.

When it comes to practicalities, suffering has much in common with evil. At the end of the previous chapter, we decided that formulating arguments about evil had its limitations. It is what one does to combat evil that really matters. In the same vein, when it comes to suffering, it is not the cleverness, or otherwise, of the arguments that count, but what one does in response to the suffering we encounter. In the end, it comes down to action rather than words. 'Is your cucumber bitter? Throw it away. Are there briars in your path? Turn aside. That is enough. Do not go on to say, "Why were things of this sort ever brought into the world?"' The advice is from Marcus Aurelius, in the second century.

Confronted by someone in distress, we are made to realize that what they need from us is help and comfort, not theoretical arguments on the meaning of suffering and how such misery might be reconciled with an all-powerful, all-knowing and supremely loving God. At that point in their lives, they might need to rail against God and cry out at the manifold injustice of what they are having to endure. Even Job, monumentally patient Job, was at one stage of his sufferings driven to cursing the day he was born. Such outpourings of despair are understandable, and God permits them. We need feel no guilt at giving vent to our feelings. But with the inner strength that comes from God, and the practical help and advice offered by doctors, counsellors, friends and relatives, one pulls through more often than not. I cannot put it better than Blaise Pascal: 'Despite the sight of all the miseries which affect us and hold us by the throat we have an irrepressible instinct which bears us up.'

PART 3

Why
Death?

Why evil? Why suffering? And now the question that perhaps looms largest of all: why death? John Galsworthy, in his novel, *A Man of Property*, introduces us to the Forsyte family: 'When a Forsyte died – but no Forsyte had as yet died; they did not die; death being contrary to their principles, they took precautions against it.' The dream of being able to cheat death continues into our own times. Woody Allen has quipped, 'I don't want to achieve immortality through my work. I want to achieve it through not dying.' I suppose the modern equivalent of 'taking precautions' is the growing practice of having one's body frozen. With further advances in medicine, the hope is that one might at some point in the future be resuscitated and thus enabled to resume life. But even were this to prove feasible, cryogenics could at most only delay the inevitable. Death is a fact; it is something we all have to face up to. And in facing it, there are those who draw the sombre conclusion that life, being transitory, must ultimately be meaningless. Are they right?

The End of Life in the Universe

Indeed, oblivion is not just the fate of us individuals. In 5,000 million years' time, the sun will swell up to become what is called a red giant star. The inner planets will be swallowed up in fire. Conditions here on earth will become bakingly hot, and all life on earth will be wiped out. The hot burning core of the sun will then shrink down and, as its nuclear fires die out, it will grow cold. The same will be true of the stars. All stars are suns like our own sun. They too in the course of time will run out of fuel. Some fizzle out tamely; others become unstable and blow up in a violent supernova explosion, their core collapsing down under its own colossal gravity forces to produce a black hole. Whatever the exact course of development the star takes, its ultimate fate is the same: it becomes a freezingly cold remnant. This is what will happen to all the stars in the universe; they die, leaving any accompanying planets cold and uninhabitable. That will be the end of *all* life everywhere. It is known as the Heat Death of the universe.

Reflecting on this scenario, Nobel Prize-winning physicist Steven Weinberg observed, 'The more the world is comprehensible, the more it also seems pointless.' He went on to dismiss life as 'a more or less farcical outcome of a chain of accidents'.

The Death of Children

The eventual, inescapable, total triumph of death throughout the entire physical world is one thought we have to contend with. Of more pressing and immediate concern, however, is our own individual death, and perhaps even more so, the problem posed by the death of children. Having ourselves lived a full life, it might not be all that difficult for us to come to terms with the prospect of having to let go. But what of children, those whose lives are cut short while young, indeed as babies? Where is the justice in that? How can there be a God of love and justice when these short lives are ended so abruptly?

The Need for a Life Beyond Death

'Death is one of two things,' pronounced Socrates. 'Either it is annihilation, and the dead have no consciousness of anything; or, as we are told, it is really a change: a migration of the soul from this place to another.'

If this life – the life we live here on earth – is all there is, then the answer to our question is simple: there is no justice, and Christian belief makes no sense, none whatsoever. What the suffering and death of small children demonstrates is that there is no room for half-baked Christianity. By that, I mean a belief that is basically Christian: Jesus was the best man who ever lived and we should all try and follow his good example and love others the way he did. But a belief that crucially falls short of accepting the resurrection, life beyond death.

That kind of religious belief just does not work. It is manifestly clear that some people in this life have a very rough time of it, no life at all worth speaking of. And here I am not thinking only of children who die young. There are many who are condemned to live out lives of unspeakable misery and privation, in total contrast to fortunate people like myself blessed with rich and fulfilling lives.

How are we to reconcile such inconsistencies? We cannot, not if we are to be restricted to taking into account only that which we see happening to these people in this earthly life. A belief in a loving God, a God of justice, can only be sustained if there is something more than this life, something better. 'Is there another life?' asked John Keats. 'Shall I awake and find this all a dream? There must be, we cannot be created for this sort of suffering.'

The Christian gospel, the 'good news', is not that Jesus was a good man who set us a fine example that we should follow. The good news is that he rose from the dead on that first Easter Sunday. In so doing, he holds out the promise that we too can share in life beyond death. That being the case, there will be opportunity for God to redress the balance, make good the injustices of this mortal life and generally put matters right. Indeed, heaven might be so wonderful, we older people on getting there could find ourselves thinking that we were the ones who were hard done by through being left down here on earth so long; according to that perspective, the lucky ones might well appear to be those who died young.

Now, of course, there are those who will dismiss such a suggestion as simply the 'jam tomorrow' scenario or 'pie in the sky when you die'. The psychologist Sigmund Freud put it down to wish-fulfilment. He claimed that if you wished for something hard enough your unconscious could trick you into believing it to be true. Thus, for example, we wish for a protective father-figure, so our unconscious leads us to believe that we have a heavenly Father. We are reluctant to accept that death marks the end of us, so we wish ourselves into a belief in life beyond death.

It sounds plausible. But is wishful thinking really the answer? If so, how come some of the greatest religious leaders of all time did not fall prey to it: Abraham, Isaac, Jacob, Moses, Isaiah, Jeremiah and Ezekiel. Indeed, none of the Jewish patriarchs had any belief that they would enjoy a life beyond death, regardless of how attractive such a prospect might have struck them. Might this not be because God at that time had yet to reveal to the world the promise of eternal life?

Jam tomorrow, and why not? What kind of pessimism takes for granted that happy endings must by their very nature be an illusion? That is not an argument; it is a prejudice. What we are trying to do in this book is examine whether Christian belief hangs together rationally in the face of the three tough questions we are considering. By this, we mean full Christian belief, not the half-baked, pick-and-mix variety. And the full set of beliefs includes a God who is a God of goodness, love, justice, and who is all-powerful. Naturally we would expect that a God like that would have not only the will but also the ability to ensure that everything works out for the best in the end. The Christian notion of resurrection, coupled with the Christian conception of the all-powerful God, makes perfect sense. One might not believe it, many do not, but such lack of belief cannot be on the grounds that it does not make sense. That is the point I am making.

Yet you might be thinking, 'Can the prospect of life beyond death really compensate for the terrible injustices and suffering some people are called upon to endure?' You might be calling to mind the worst excesses of the Nazis during the Holocaust. How can a life hereafter possibly compensate for the intense suffering that some people had to undergo? Intense their suffering undoubtedly was, but one thing we must not lose sight of: the suffering was finite; it came to an end. Life beyond death, on the other hand, is infinite. There is no comparing the finite with the infinite.

Belief in Life Beyond Death

It is one thing to assert that there needs to be something beyond this life for the idea of a God of love and justice to be sustained, but do we actually believe there is something of that nature?

Surveys carried out in the UK show that about half the population have such a belief, the remainder either don't know or reject the notion. The proportion of believers is lower in certain other European countries and in Japan, and higher in the USA. Such statistics appear to be cut-and-dried, but in truth, when probing in depth what an individual actually believes, one often finds their attitudes are much more ambiguous and inconsistent.

Take, for example, the case of a work

colleague of mine who tragically lost his young wife. I was deeply touched when he asked me if I would conduct her funeral. I readily agreed. But then he hurriedly added that both he and his wife were atheists; the ceremony, he insisted, would have to be non-religious. I thought for a moment, but then I replied that if that is what he wanted, I was still prepared to do it. I even agreed to his demand that the cross be removed from the wall of the crematorium chapel, though I personally felt that the gesture was taking things to unnecessary extremes.

The ceremony, as I had discussed with him beforehand, was a simple one based on the idea of thanksgiving; it consisted of extracts from his wife's favourite readings and music, together with testimonials from friends and family members. There was no mention of God. It all seemed to pass off to everyone's satisfaction.

At the reception afterwards, one of the guests approached me and expressed puzzlement as to why the widower, who was so militantly atheist, had asked me, someone known for his religious beliefs, to preside over the ceremony. I replied that she would have to work that one out for herself. But then she went on to enquire how I, as a religious person, had felt about conducting such an atheistic ceremony. I replied that I did not see it as atheistic. We were giving thanks. But you can't give thanks unless you are thanking *someone*. Were we thanking the deceased, or were we thanking God? According to the atheistic point of view, it is too late to thank the deceased, and there is no God. So the ceremony, if truly an atheistic one, made no sense.

Resurrection of the Body

If self-avowed atheists can sometimes adopt confused and inconsistent attitudes over what they really believe, that is nothing compared to some of the confusions to be found among religious believers. Take, for example, the statement in the creed that says, 'I believe in the resurrection of the body.' The *body*? How can that be? How is God supposed to get all the pieces of a person's body back together again once it has decomposed and been eaten by worms, or when it has been cremated?

The answer is that this is not what the creed has in mind. It is not a question of bringing back together the atoms of the old body. Rather, it is asserting that in the life to come we shall each of us retain our own personal identity; we shall not be absorbed into some kind of anonymous, homogenized spiritual 'soup'. I shall still be recognizable as me and you as you.

Then why talk about 'resurrection of the body'? Well, how do we recognize each other in this life? It is through our physical bodies. I recognize you from your appearance, the sound of your voice, your *physical* voice, and so on. And that is how it will be in the next life. We shall each have a body. Not this body, not a physical body, but a body of some kind. It is rather like an encyclopedia. An encyclopedia might be in the form of books, a whole shelf full of books; or it could be in the form of a CD. All that information, exactly the same information, repackaged in a different form. That is how it will be with us in respect to the life beyond death. Each of us might be regarded as a bundle of information. At present, that information is packaged as a physical body. But it doesn't have to be. It can be passed on and reassembled in different form. Don't ask me in what form; I don't know. But some form, and whatever it is we call it, a 'body', a spiritual body.

Not only do we have to be vague about the form of that body, we also should not expect to know how God will bring about this transformation. We do not even know how God managed to create us in the first place, in this present physical form. That was surely the difficult part: creating something, the whole world, from nothing. And yet he managed to do it. Resurrection might be regarded as 'merely' recreating in different form what has already been created.

When we lose a loved one, we mourn their loss; we grieve for them; we keep alive the memory of them. So it is we ask, 'If God, in his infinite love for us, were to lose his loved ones, would he not mourn; would he not keep the memory of us alive?' Except that here, we are talking of a memory in the mind of God, the mind of the Ground of All Being. Would not the very act of God remembering us automatically invest us with an existence of some kind? We grieve for our lost loved ones. God has no need to grieve; he can do something about it.

An intriguing thought: God will be remembering us not just as we were at the time of our death, but he will be calling to mind our entire life story. Might not God therefore be able to invest our resurrection body with that complete life story, not just its ending? I have always been more than a little disturbed at the thought of there being so many old folk like myself up there. Perhaps it is not like that. Perhaps our childhood and adolescence were not mere staging posts along the way to the goal of becoming an adult. Our childhood had value in itself, and for God it might continue to do so. (Indeed, he might prefer us the way we were, rather than what we later became!) I have always suspected that, in a sense, we never grow up. In adulthood, the child in us merely acts the role of an adult. The games might be somewhat more elaborate and the toys more expensive, but they are games and toys nonetheless. Jesus did say that to enter the kingdom of heaven we must become as little children. We might find that in heaven we shall be called upon to lay aside the adult masks we assumed in this life and join a more childlike community.

The Prospect of Heaven

What else might one say about life in heaven? Not a lot. Medieval artists were constantly being commissioned by churches to depict heavenly scenes. They seem to have been notably short on imagination, being content to depict hosts of saints and angels adoring Christ and the Virgin Mary. As one art historian put it, 'There seems to be a lot of standing around doing nothing.' George Bernard Shaw put it more bluntly: 'Heaven, as conventionally conceived, is a place so inane, so dull, so useless, so miserable, that nobody has ventured to describe a whole day in heaven, though plenty of people have described a day at the seaside.'

How do I personally see heaven? I am one of those who likes to get on with things. If I am on holiday, I rush around doing the sights, rather than laze around in the sunshine on a beach. Most days I make out a list of tasks and jobs to be done. I get satisfaction from progressively ticking off the items as they are finished. I get enormous satisfaction from completing some major project, like writing a book. So my idea of heaven would be to arrive at the pearly gates and have St Peter confront me, saying, 'Thank goodness you're here. Where have you been? God has this list of jobs for you to be getting on with – and you are already behind schedule.' Great! I would know what I had to do.

But it will not be like that. I recall a retirement party being thrown for one of my colleagues. I asked him what he planned to be doing now that he was retired. 'Do?' he replied. 'I am not going to *do* anything; I am going to *be*.' I suspect heaven will be like that: more about *being* than *doing*. Which raises the spectre of heaven being boring, not just for us non-musicians consigned to 'standing around doing nothing', but even for those chosen to play the harps – forever. 'Eternity is a terrible thought. I mean, where's it going to end?' wrote Tom Stoppard.

Except that it will not be like that either. Being bored takes time, lots of time, and as far as we know, heaven is neither in time nor space. That is why it is preferable to speak of eternal life rather than everlasting life. The term 'everlasting' clearly indicates duration, an unceasing span of time; 'eternal', on the other hand, has among its meanings a sense of timelessness: no beginning or ending, immutability.

Which brings us up against an insoluble problem: we creatures of time and space simply cannot imagine a timeless and spaceless existence. The theologian Hans Küng writes, 'The new life remains something for which we can hope, but which is beyond our vision or imagination… Language here reaches its limits.' And that is why, where heaven is concerned, we must ultimately be patient until we have the experience of it directly. 'At the moment of death, I hope to be surprised,' wrote the Austrian-born theologian, Ivan Illich. I am sure we shall all be surprised.

All we can really venture to say about the life beyond is that there will be a deep sense of the presence of God, an awareness much richer and more direct than that which most of us are capable

of achieving in this life. The fuller revelation
of God's glory and splendour will doubtless be
accompanied by much joy, warmth and love. In
fact, I can do no better than quote from Sir Walter
Scott's *Lay of the Last Minstrel*:

Love rules the court, the camp, the grove,
and men below and saints above;
For love is heaven, and heaven is love.

The Prospect of Hell

So much for the pleasant prospect of eternal life
in the presence of God in heaven. But what of the
Other Place? The subject of hell opens up a whole
can of worms, if we are to take seriously the
description of it given in Isaac Watts's hymn,
'Heaven and Hell':

There is a dreadful hell,
  and everlasting pains:
there sinners must with devils dwell
  in darkness, fire, and chains.

Can we really reconcile the idea of a loving God
with that? Are we to think of God as a deity who
deliberately punishes and tortures people in hell,
for eternity, without that person being able to do
anything about it, because it is too late? A God
of revenge, indeed, of sadism? It is hard not to
sympathize with the view expressed by British
politician John Morley, when he spoke of hell as

116

'The most frightful idea that has ever corroded human nature – the idea of eternal punishment.'

Jesus refers to hell in three different ways. He says, 'fear him who is able to destroy both body and soul in hell'. So the emphasis here is on destruction, on ceasing to exist. Second, he talks of being cast into outer darkness, in other words being excluded, banished, not able to join in the joys of heaven. Third, he does talk of hell as everlasting punishment.

But to be destroyed or to be banished would in themselves be punishment. It is not a case of God deliberately torturing people. That surely would be out of character with a loving God. The language of hell-fire is not so much to do with the infliction of pain as being a symbol of destruction – it is a destroying fire, a means of ending something. Both Paul in his letters and John in his Gospel go no further than to say that unbelievers will 'perish'.

Hell is a self-inflicted penalty. By living a life in which one has turned one's back on the loving God, there is nothing in heaven that the sinner can connect with or identify with. The sheer essence of heaven is building on that loving relationship begun on earth, at last seeing God face to face. The sinner, on the other hand, has nothing to build on. The hell he finds himself in is one of his own making. God doesn't sadistically gloat over this, or anything of that kind. He grieves over it. It was his wish that everyone should have used their earthly lives to get to know him. But he is powerless to stop people voluntarily choosing to make a hell of their own, a hell that many of them seem to be in already, this side of the grave. John Milton put his finger on it in *Paradise Lost*, when he wrote,

The mind is its own place, and in itself
can make a heaven of hell, a hell of heaven.

Life Beyond Death in Other Religions

This book is primarily concerned with Christian belief; it is the only faith I know about in any depth. One has to live a faith in order to really get to understand it, and for the individual this can only be done in respect of a single religion. Yet one cannot help but notice some of the things other religions have to say about subjects such as life beyond death. Belief that there is more to life than this earthly existence is not the prerogative of Christianity alone.

Such a belief has its roots in ancient history. One has only to think of the custom whereby possessions were buried along with the bodies of the dead. These were obviously intended for use by the deceased in the life to come.

In the early parts of the Bible, as we have already noted, it appears the Jewish people did not believe in life beyond death, not life for the individual. There was talk of going to Sheol (meaning 'no-land'), but that was not a place of punishment like hell or reward like heaven. Everyone went there, the righteous as well as the wicked, the rich rulers and the poor peasants, all reduced to the same level. It wasn't exactly oblivion either. It was a separation from life and from God – a kind of miserable lingering memory.

It is only in the later writings, beginning with the book of Daniel (written about 160 BC), that the idea of immortality for the individual begins to take shape. Certain outstanding individuals, Enoch and Elijah, had been spoken of as having been taken up into heaven without having to die. But now the idea of there being life beyond death for many others began to take root, probably in response to the conviction that God is a God of justice, and therefore there was a need to square that with the problem of martyrs, those who had died for their belief in that God.

But even up to the time of Jesus, there was still much doubt about this, particularly among the group known as the Sadducees. There was the tendency for Jews to see themselves living on in their children, passing on their characteristics and continuing to live on in the memories of future generations, in the same way as they themselves had in their own time kept in remembrance those who had gone before them.

According to Islam, life is a time of trial by good and by evil. It is a time for us to return to the straight path laid down by God. Death is no punishment, but merely the end of this time of testing. When one is dead, one will be asked by two angels, 'Whom have you worshipped? And who is your prophet?' If they answer Allah and Muhammad, they rest until the Day of Judgment.

But those who have rejected God and Muhammad will immediately be punished.

On the Day of Judgment, everyone will be rewarded according to an exact reckoning. Yet it will not be purely through deeds that one will attain salvation, but through the mercy of Allah shown to those who repent this side of death.

Hindus, as we noted earlier, believe in rebirth, the self being reborn repeatedly, perhaps coming back next time as an animal, sometimes coming back as something better. Each rebirth reflects how one has lived one's previous lives. There is a way of escape from this endless chain of rebirths. It can be achieved through appropriate actions. But that does not mean devoting more and more energy to them. One has to develop a sense of detachment. It is the performance of the actions themselves that is one's proper business, not attachment to their possible fruits. The death one currently faces is of no great moment. It is only one of many deaths we have to pass through. Each death is but a staging post to the next life. As a Hindu, one must not persist in mourning and grieving over the dead.

In Buddhism, there is no continuing existence of the self after death. Does that mean death is extinction or oblivion? No. There is continuity of consequence even though there is no rebirth of a self, no continuing subject of experience that goes from life to life. The process of life is like the successive frames of a film, with each individual frame giving rise to the next. A continuous story is being told, but by a succession of distinctive frames; it is not a single frame repeating itself in slightly different guises. But although the frames are individual, they do have within them the marks of the consequences of the previous ones in the sequence. That is why the Buddha and others are able to recall past existences.

This continuity eventually comes to an end in the condition known as nirvana. It is a cessation, a negation of desire, of lust, of affection, of thirst, of longing. It is the end of craving. As such it is the highest happiness. One does not have to die to attain nirvana. The Buddha attained nirvana in his Enlightenment.

It is not surprising that the main religions come up with different ideas as to what lies beyond death: resurrection, rebirth, or whatever. No one living has had direct experience of it – obviously. We have to infer what it might be like from this life; we must use our imagination. What is remarkable is that, with the exception of Buddhism (but not *all* forms of Buddhism, for example, that which developed in Tibet), the major religions, Eastern and Western, are agreed that there is something about us as individuals that extends beyond death, a persistence of identity, and the quality of that extension of life depends to some extent on how we live this life. Death marks a transition, not an end, and as such is not to be feared.

An Alternative to Death?

And yet we do fear it. Not everyone, of course. There are those who have lived a full life and have now reached old age with its accompanying afflictions and infirmities, and who feel quite simply that they have had enough. One recalls in this connection the words of W. Somerset Maugham on the occasion of his ninetieth birthday: 'I am sick of this way of life. The weariness and sadness of old age make it intolerable. I have walked with death in hand, and death's own hand is warmer than my own. I don't wish to live any longer.' Then there are those who find life so unbearable, black despair drives them to commit suicide. Such tragedies do occur – as my own family has learned to its cost.

But having said that, the vast majority of us value our lives, and we do our very best to try and stay alive. Indeed, the prospect of death casts a sombre shadow over us. 'Death is someone you see very clearly with eyes in the center of your heart: eyes that see not by reacting to light, but by reacting to a kind of chill from within the marrow of your own life,' wrote the American religious writer Thomas Merton.

This being so, it is natural to ask whether God could not have arranged things differently, given us a life that was not to be ended in death, a life that did not need to be transformed through death into another. By way of an answer, let us suppose for a moment that there was indeed no such thing as death. What would be the consequences of that?

The knowledge that one has to die concentrates the mind wonderfully. The fact that life is short means that we pay more attention to the way we live it, which we would not do to the same degree if time were unlimited. We all know of people who continually put things off until tomorrow. We might be guilty of that ourselves. Certainly I found that when I lived in London, I never seemed to get around to visiting all the sights that visitors came from miles around to see. When it is on your doorstep, and you can pop in and see them at any time, what's the hurry? What is so special about going to see it today rather than some other time? The result – one never goes at all. It is only since I moved out of the capital, that I have come to savour my visits there, packing in as many activities as possible in the limited time available.

The same thing happened when I officially retired from work. A senior citizen? ME!? I don't mind telling you, that brought me up short. Faced with my own mortality, I found myself, as a matter of urgency, reviewing what else I wanted to do with my life – before it was too late.

Without death, the older generations would never get out of the way to make room for the younger. The younger would always live in their shadow. They would never gain promotion at work and progress their careers because all the top jobs would already be filled – permanently. They would have no opportunity to take on responsibility and become mature. The world would get very crowded.

A world without death would be one where

we could never make the ultimate sacrifice on behalf of another: 'For greater love hath no man than this, that he lay down his life for his friends.'

Without death we humans would not be here in the first place. We are the products of evolution by natural selection, crudely speaking, 'the survival of the fittest'. But in a world without death, *all* would survive, not just those fortunate enough to be endowed with beneficial characteristics that contribute towards adaptation to one's surroundings and conditions. Without the weeding-out process that works against the perpetuation of less beneficial characteristics, there would have been no development. Death of the individual, and of whole species, had to be an integral feature of the process that led to the emergence of humankind. The premature death of those not endowed with the beneficial characteristics was inescapable. And not only that, but the ultimate death of even those who did possess the beneficial characteristics was necessary (once those characteristics had been passed on to their offspring), so as to make way for the next and more highly developed generation. Without death, there could have been no evolution.

A Death Gene?

Death had such an important part to play in the process, it is believed that there might well be something about our genetic make-up that ensures we eventually age and die, and just get out of the way. Which raises a fascinating question. You will doubtless have heard of the Human Genome Project – that vast undertaking mapping out all the components of the human genetic make-up. Suppose scientists were one day to identify the characteristic responsible for ageing and death. What ought they to do about it? Ought it to be regarded as somehow defective, like the known gene inducing sickle-cell anaemia? Should a policy be adopted of eradicating it as a therapeutic measure? Or ought it to be regarded as natural, as an integral, healthy part of our genetic make-up? Should death be regarded as an integral feature of life itself? As Dag Hammarskjöld reminds us, 'In the last analysis, it is our conception of death which decides our answers to all the questions that life puts to us.' The American writer Saul Bellow expresses it like this: 'Death is the dark backing a mirror needs if we are to see anything.'

Evidence for Life Beyond Death

So much for evolution and the necessity of death. Let us return to the question of what, if anything, lies beyond death. What evidence is there for it?

Some people claim to have seen ghosts, departed spirits that linger on or visit us from other realms. I personally have no such experience to draw upon. Perhaps you have.

I think some people need to 'see' ghosts; they need to interact with their departed loved ones for emotional reasons, to complete unfinished business, get things sorted out. It is part of the grieving process. Cutting the ties does not necessarily happen all at once. Those left behind have to get used to being on their own, and that can take a while. 'People do not die for us immediately, but remain bathed in a sort of aura of life which bears no relation to true immortality but through which they continue to occupy our thoughts in the same way as when they were alive,' said Marcel Proust. Seeing a ghost and talking with it might be part of that healing process. Whether it is all a product of the imagination, who is to say?

Then there are those who try to contact the dead through a medium, perhaps in the course of a seance. The vast majority of mediums are undoubtedly fakes, and most so-called seances are just a bit of fairground fun. But again, whether there is exceptionally any residue of real contact with the dead, it is hard to say.

Then there are the accounts of near-death experiences, such as for example, the sense of hovering over the hospital bed and viewing oneself from above, or being drawn through a tunnel to a light, or experiencing a sense of reassurance.

Each of us has to make up our own minds as to whether there is likely to be anything in any of these indications of something beyond death.

But for Christians the clearest indication of life beyond death is likely to come from Christ's resurrection, both the reports of it in the Bible and the experience of 'meeting' the risen Christ in one's prayer life. The latter type of encounter can be so convincing that it becomes a matter of secondary importance as to whether Jesus did, as a matter of historical record, physically rise from the dead – whether the tomb was empty. But for others, the events of that first Easter Day are regarded as crucial. That being so, let us take a little time to examine the evidence.

In the first place, there are those who dismiss the whole story as a fabrication put about by the disciples. Indeed, there was at the time a rumour encouraged by the high priests that the disciples had themselves stolen the body and concocted this tale of Jesus coming back to life. It is hard to see why the disciples would have done any such thing. Generally speaking at the time there was no great expectation that one survived death, so they would have been only too aware that a story like that would have been greeted with incredulity and derision. It is not as though there was any expectation that the Messiah would rise from the dead, so the claim would not have added to Jesus' credentials in that regard. So there appears to be no motive.

Then again, consider the type of people who were supposed to be doing the lying. These were not practised liars – far from it. Can anyone doubt that at heart the disciples were decent, honest folk? Indeed, the conspiracy, if such it was, would not only have involved the disciples but also the women who knew Jesus, and the crowd of 500 who saw him. Can one really believe that, if all these people had really colluded together to cook up this cock-and-bull story, not a single person would have subsequently talked, even under the intense pressures brought to bear on them?

What about the reports of the events as recorded in the Bible? They purport to be eyewitness accounts of events that actually happened. Do they read that way? Do they pass the common tests applied these days by police to check the validity of so-called eyewitness accounts of, say, accidents or crimes?

In the first place, the accounts are not in the form of a carefully rehearsed, tidy account of the main points we need to know. Those main points are mixed up with inconsequential details. One wonders whether the witness will ever get to the point! Who, for example, needs to know that of the two disciples who ran to the tomb, the one who reached it first did not go in straightaway but waited for the other to catch up and it was the second disciple who entered first. Who cares? Presumably it is included because that happens to be the way it was.

Second, one notes that with true eyewitness accounts, moments of shock are remembered particularly vividly; it is almost as though the witness is describing a scene that is still etched into their mind. The account of the scene that confronted the disciples in the empty tomb, with the cloth that had been round Jesus' head lying a little apart from the main wrapping, is described in just such graphic detail.

Then there are the inconsistencies that are only to be expected between the accounts given by different witnesses. Where, for instance, were Jesus' subsequent appearances? According to Matthew and Mark they took place in Galilee; Luke has them confined to Jerusalem; while John has them occurring in both locations. If we are dealing with a conspiracy, one would have thought they would have got their story straight.

Then there are those instances that crop up where the witness has difficulty accounting for various aspects of their own behaviour, lapses that might leave them looking a little foolish. Why, for instance, did Mary in the garden outside the tomb mistake Jesus for the gardener? How come the two disciples on the road to Emmaus could be in deep conversation with Jesus, invite him into the place they were staying and begin a meal with him without recognizing who it was? Made-up stories tend to be much neater than that.

Then there is the remarkable omission of any description of the resurrection itself, Jesus triumphantly emerging from the tomb in glory. Can one seriously imagine that a fabricated story of a resurrection would omit the central, crucial event itself? Surely not.

Then finally we need to draw attention to a further aspect of the behaviour of the disciples. At the time of the crucifixion, they had all fled; they were frightened, dejected and hiding from the authorities behind closed doors. Again, if we are dealing with a made-up story, is it likely they would have revealed themselves in such a poor light? Then suddenly they are out and about in the streets, deliriously happy, ready to die for the cause. Something amazing must have happened to bring that about. A bunch of cowards doesn't suddenly start behaving like that because they have made up a fairy story. And note that they were joyful. It wasn't a case of being angry and resentful about the unfair way their leader had been put to death, which is what one might have expected. They were not demanding justice or revenge on the people that had perpetrated the crime. No. The crucifixion was a thing of the past; now they were happy, they were celebrating what they saw as a great victory. Something had happened, and whatever it was, it had brought about a quite stunning transformation.

So what does one conclude? It seems pretty clear to me that the Gospel accounts have all the hallmarks expected of genuine eyewitness accounts. There is also no motive I can see why anyone would have made up such an unlikely story. The evidence, such as it is, could hardly be improved upon. After all, suppose you and I were in a room with some others, and all of a sudden Winston Churchill walked through the wall, talked to us about his war experiences, had a meal with us, handed out cigars, puffed the smoke in our faces and then promptly vanished. How would we go about convincing anyone who had not been present on this extraordinary occasion of what had happened? It would not be easy – to put it mildly. No matter how hard we tried, in the end we would have to rely on those other people taking our word for it. And that is how it is with the resurrection. Having done our best to test for the likely authenticity of the biblical accounts, and having noted the transformation wrought in the lives of the disciples, even to the extent that they were now prepared to suffer martyrdom for the truth of what they were saying, the remaining gap has to be spanned by an act of faith.

This act of faith need not be as great as one might think. I go back to what I said earlier about us being able to meet the risen Jesus directly, in our prayer life. Those who believe they are truly interacting with a Jesus who is alive here and now, such people believe in the resurrection, in life beyond death. And this is regardless of what they might feel able to accept about what actually, physically occurred on the first Easter Day. As Hans Küng has written, 'Neither Jesus' resurrection nor ours is dependent on an empty tomb. The reanimation of a corpse is not a precondition for rising to eternal life... Christian faith therefore appeals not to the empty tomb but to the encounter with the living Christ himself: "Why look among the dead for someone who is alive?"'

Death – the Taboo Subject

Although one might accept wholeheartedly the idea of life beyond death, death itself can, nevertheless, retain its power to frighten and disturb us. We still have to cope with death, to come to terms with it. And it is here we find we get little help from our modern-day society.

On the face of it, we are confronted by death all the time. Our children spend hours playing computer games where the intention is to kill the enemy. Our TV screens are constantly conveying to us pictures of disasters, warfare, massacres, murders, people dying of starvation and so on. At one level, we are constantly being reminded of death. But it is only at a superficial level. The video games and the violent movies are manifestly not real. Even the news bulletins do not strike home to us the way they ought. The deaths shown there are always happening somewhere else and to people we do not know. We are not drawn into and bound up in the reality of those deaths.

When it comes to death on our own doorstep, the deaths that really do matter to us, we observe for the most part a conspiracy of silence. We live in a society where most of us are allowed to get on with our lives as though death is not something that is ever likely to happen to *us*.

It was not so in the past. Then it was a case of just about every family being afflicted by the deaths of babies and young children. Not only that, there was the ever-present threat of plague and other untreatable diseases. Death was not something one could sweep under the carpet and pretend would not happen.

Nowadays, it is simply not done to talk about death. Even if someone is on their deathbed, and everyone knows that to be the case, the very last person they are likely to talk to about the impending death is the patient.

This wall of silence gives rise to a false perspective on life. We expect, as of right, to live to a ripe old age; if we get ill we expect doctors to have the means of curing us. If they don't, we consider this an outrage. Living life as though it is going to go on forever, we are in danger of devaluing the precious twenty-four hours given to us each day. The only way to appreciate life to the full is to live each day as though it were our last.

We have noted that most of us have a fear of death. And yet, as the Reverend Sydney Smith warned, 'Death must be distinguished from dying, with which it is often confounded.' Is it death we fear or the act of dying? The latter can be unpleasant – not always of course, but in some cases it involves pain and discomfort. 'Death is not so serious. Pain is,' declared the French writer André Malraux. Fear of dying is nothing to be ashamed of. Even Jesus himself, on the night he was betrayed, prayed to be spared, even though he presumably did not fear the state of being dead, knowing that he was to be raised by his Father in heaven.

If it is natural to be apprehensive about the manner in which we might have to die, it is also understandable to feel sadness and to grieve over the loss of loved ones. But even here it is important to identify what one is being sorry about. We are being sorry for ourselves. We are the ones who will now have to cope without the love, help and presence of the deceased. There is some truth in Thomas Mann's assertion that 'a man's dying is more the survivors' affair than his own'. We are not being sorry for the person who has died. Why should we? They have gone to heaven to be with their Maker. For that reason, in certain churches, a funeral is treated as a happy occasion, with lots of cheerful, upbeat music and singing. It is not a time for grieving for ourselves but of celebrating. It is a celebration of a good life lived.

Death of the Universe

Finally, what shall we say of the prospect of the universality of death throughout the physical cosmos when all the suns run out of fuel, their fires are extinguished, and their accompanying planets grow cold and lifeless? Is this the final triumph of death?

Not so. If we regard this mortal life as being, in the words of Keats, but 'a vale of soul-making', the universe will by then have served its purpose;

it will have provided the temporary home required for spiritual beings like ourselves to grow and develop. Its task successfully completed, it can now subside gently into a well-earned everlasting rest; we on the other hand are destined for eternal life.

Concluding Remarks

And that is as much as I have to say on the subject of why a good, all-powerful, loving God allows evil, suffering and death in the world he has created. Looking back I realize how inadequate my contribution has been; I seem merely to have scratched the surface.

Who knows, perhaps we, and everyone else who has ever addressed this problem, have got it all wrong. Perhaps the question we have been asking was not the right one. As a scientist, I am only too aware that the truly great scientific discoveries and insights come not so much from finally discovering the answer to the question everyone has been asking, as from the recognition that there was something wrong with the question itself. Though it might have seemed a sensible, obvious sort of question at the time, it is revealed later to be quite meaningless. We discover that we were looking at the problem from the wrong angle. The solution lay in adopting a totally different perspective, one based on alternative initial assumptions. Whether this will prove to be the case over the question we have been considering here, I don't know.

One thing is certain: as with all intellectual debates, our discussion has tended to be cut and dried, logical, disinterested, in short, academic. Which for most topics is fair enough. But when dealing with suffering, such arguments, as I have said before, come across as unfeelingly clever-clever – no help at all when it comes to the more pressing problem of how to cope with suffering, or with the consequences of evil, or the prospect of impending death. Indeed, I cannot stress too highly that what we have been engaged in is philosophy, *not* religion. Philosophy deals in ideas; religion is more concerned with the living out of a practical, pastoral life stemming from a felt relationship of love for God and for one's fellow creatures. The danger of the sort of discussion we have been engaged in is that we might end up content in the knowledge that we have discovered some grounds why a measure of evil and suffering is necessary in this world; why it was meant to be. Philosophically speaking, that might be true. But in practical terms, that must never lull us into thinking that we should therefore sit back and accept them as an inevitable feature of the world God 'intended'. Suffering might be necessary, but it is also intended that we try to alleviate it wherever possible, and where that proves not possible, to help the sufferer to be reconciled to their plight. As for evil, that must at all times be fought; it is not something to which we can ever be reconciled. This is so whether the evil is in others or in our own selves. It is not for nothing Christian worship usually begins with an act of confession and a new resolve to live more closely to God's ways in future.

Let me end by reminding ourselves of the

sheer enormity of what we have been attempting. As I said in the Introduction, suffering is ultimately a mystery. William Wordsworth expressed it in the words:

Suffering is permanent, obscure and dark,
and shares the nature of infinity.

We can talk about suffering, argue about it, and try to rationalize about it. But in the end, we have to admit that a fully satisfactory solution eludes our grasp – and always will do.

Should we limited creatures have ever expected to be able to understand everything? Hardly. We cannot even understand why our fellow human beings sometimes act the way they do, or even on occasion why we ourselves have behaved as we did. How little then can we expect to understand the workings of the mind of God. In the sight of God, we are but children. How often are children bewildered by, not to say resentful of, the discipline laid upon them by their parents? In later life, he or she might be able to look back with the benefit of hindsight and see the good that came out of being forced to clean one's teeth, not live on a diet of chocolate, take nasty-tasting medicine when ill, go to bed at a set time, do one's homework and so on. But at the time it was simply a case of getting on with it, trusting that one's parents were acting in a loving, caring way.

So it is with us and God. A God who was fully comprehensible to the human mind would be but a product of the human mind. It is the fact that we do not fully understand God that testifies to his independent reality. God is not the sort of God one would have readily dreamt up out of one's own imagination; he is too paradoxical for that.

Something of the mystery and incomprehensibility of God is vividly captured in the book of Job. Job was a good man, and yet he had to suffer terribly. His so-called comforters were determined to come up with a simple, neat, rational explanation for all the calamities that had befallen him. Thus, so they claimed, he must have sinned badly, this being his just punishment. But Job knew that could not possibly be the answer. In the end, he came face to face with God. He had demanded an explanation for his troubles. At this point in the story, we are thinking that at last we are about to get the answer straight from the mouth of God. But it is not to be. Instead of an answer, Job himself is bombarded with questions from God – over fifty of them – all designed to expose how little he and other humans know about anything. In the end, Job can do nothing but humbly accept that ultimately suffering is beyond human understanding. It is something we must bear patiently, trusting that the loving, all-powerful God has his reasons, and that he will, in his own time and in his own way, ensure that all will be well. We must learn to accept that suffering is necessary, to the extent that God himself suffered on the cross. If God himself could find no alternative to suffering, we can take it that there is no alternative; it is inevitable. The best that God can do – and it is a wonderful best – is to share the suffering with us and triumph over it. He is in the thick of it with us, assuring us, through the resurrection of Jesus, that this is the way to ultimate victory and the accomplishment of his purposes.

Then Job replied to the Lord: 'You asked, "Who is this that obscures my counsel without knowledge?" Surely I spoke of things I did not understand, things too wonderful for me to know.'

JOB 42:1, 3